The Sadness of Autumn

P9-CKG-716

The Sadness of Autumn

BY

CANON SHEEHAN

THE MERCIER PRESS

CORK and DUBLIN

THE MERCIER PRESS, 4 Bridge Street, Cork
25 Lower Abbey Street, Dublin 1

This edition 1973

SBN 85342 329 6

PUBLISHERS NOTE

the Cedars and the Stars. The remaining parts are published under the following titles:
shed under the following titles:

The Loneliness of Winter

The Magic of Spring

The Beauty of Summer

CONTENTS

SECTION I

SECTION II

SECTION III

Fénelon – Lacordaire – The Curé of Ars – Lamennais – The latent power of the priesthood – Irreverence – Reverence – The Pearl of great price – The excellence of Philosophy – Ancient Rome imported its philosophy – The Greek Fathers – Cycles of Thought – Adumbrations of Christianity – The Gospel, the Term of all philosophies – A friendly Robin – His song – Keats – 'Mad Shelley' – His philanthropy – A singular union – The fall of the leaf – Behind the veil – The Future, unknown and merciful – The death of Nature – Its skeleton framework – A little child – The form of a slave – The Temples of the Holy Ghost – The Word was made Flesh. pp. 67-93

SECTION I.

My Garden

This is its great, its only merit. It is a *hortus conclusus, et disseptus*. Three high walls bound it, north, south, and west; and on the east are lofty stables, effectually shutting out all possibility of being seen by too curious eyes. It is a secluded spot, and in one particular angle, at the western end, it is walled in by high trees and shrubs, and you see only leafage and grasses, and the eye of God looking through the interminable azure. The monks' gardens bound it on the northern side; and here in the long summer evenings, I hear the brothers chanting in alternate strophes the Rosary of Mary. The sounds come over and through my garden wall, and they are muffled into a sweet, dreamy monotone of musical prayer. But the monks never look over my boundaries, because they are incurious, and because there is not much to be seen. For I cannot employ a professional gardener, and it is my own very limited knowledge, but great love for flowers – 'the sweetest things God has made, and forgot to put a soul in' – and the obedient handiwork of a humble labourer, that keep my garden always clean and bright, and some are kind enough to say, beautiful. And we have sycamores, and pines, and firs; and laburnum, and laurel, and lime, and lilac; and my garden is buried, deep as a well, beneath dusky walls of forest trees, beeches and elms and oaks, that rival in sublimity and altitude their classic brethren of Lebanon, leaving but the tiniest margin of blue mountain, stretching sierra-like between them and the stars.

But my garden is something more to me. It is my *Stoa* –
my porch, where some unseen teacher ever speaks, as if
with voice authoritative. It is to me the grove of Aca-
deme. Here, under the laburnum, or the solitary lime
or sycamore, I walk with spirits quite as wise as those
who trod the ancient groves with Plato, and questioned
him sharply, and drew out his wonderful dialectical
powers. But my spirits question not. They are no sophists, weaving subtleties out of the web and woof of
dainty words; nor do they ask *why* and *wherefore*. They
only speak by their silence, and answer my interroga-
tions. For I am an inquisitive being, and the mystery
of the world weighs heavily upon me. I have the faculty
of wonder strangely developed. An ephemera, floating
in the summer air; a worm creeping from cave to cave
in the warm, open earth; the pink tips of a daisy's
fingers make me glad with surprise. Miracles are all
around me, and I take them literally, and wonder at
them. *Omnia admirari!* is my motto; I have not steeled
myself into the stoicism, that can see worlds overturned
– with a shrug. I have a child's wonder, and a child's
love.

Its Time-keeper

For example, I want to know who is the time-keeper
and warden and nightwatchman of my flowers. It is not
the sun, because they are awake before the sun, and
long after his rays slant high above their heads. It is
not light, because whilst it is yet light, light enough to
read with ease and pleasure, behold, my little flowers
close their eyes ever so softly and silently, as if they

feared to disturb the harmonies of Nature; and as if they would say: 'We are such little things, never mind us! We are going to sleep, for we are so tiny and humble, why should we keep watch and ward over the mighty Universe?' And again, who has bidden my crocuses wake up from their wintry sleep, whilst the frost is on the grass, and the snow is yet hiding in the corners of the garden beds? And here, my little snowdrop, so pure and fragile, braves the keen arrows of frost and sleet, and pushes its pure blossoms out of the iron earth! This is the bulb of a hyacinth; this, the bulb of a gladiolus or a dahlia. But the former wakes up in early spring, and hangs its sweet bells on the pure virgin air; while the latter sleeps on through the cold of Spring and the blazing heat of Summer, and only wakes up when all Nature is dying around, and seems to be calling, calling for another proof of its immortality. Who is the watchman of the flowers? Who holds his timepiece in his hands, and says: 'Sleep on, O dahlia! sleep, though Spring should call for universal allegiance, and Summer winds challenge thee to resurrection; but awake, narcissus, and tremble at thine own beauty!' It is not the atmosphere. The Spring might be warm, and the Autumn chilly; or *vice versa*. It is not temperature, for the most fragile things flourish in the cold. What is it? Who hath marked their times and seasons, and warns them when their hour hath struck? Who but Thou, great Warden of the Universe?

The Law of Expansion and Repression

Yet, whatever be said of times and seasons, which the Father has placed in His own power, I perceive that there is implanted in all being, even in these tiny flowers,

11

a principle, a law, which appears to be universal. That law is what may be called the centrifugal force of being, or the power and tendency to expansion. Wherever it is localized, there it is – the universal and uniform impulse of everything to get outside itself, to enlarge its sphere of being, to develop its potencies, to become other than it is. It is true of the nebula, which is ever broadening and deepening, until by perpetual accretions it grows into a sun: it is true of the acorn, that yearns to become and oak; of the bulb that is ambitious to become a flower. And again is there a counter law, that by some hidden, irresistible force is equally bent on repressing this impulse, and destroying it. Expansion means repression. For the solitary, innate force that seeks to develop or reproduce, there are a hundred external forces that try to suspend or check that evolution. When my beautiful gladiolus comes forth, painted in all lovely colours, – saffron tinged with red, or purple streaked with gold – everything around will conspire to destroy the loveliness. And the moment a nebula rounds its sidereal fires into a central sun, all its sister suns will seek to drag it into the cauldrons of their own terrific fires; it will be pelted by vagrant comets, and stoned with fiery meteors; and that Hercules of the heavens, that invisible giant, Gravitation, will drag it hither and thither, and force its centrifugal and expansive powers into the training circles of the Universe.

Applied to Genius

And weep not, O thou child of genius, if obeying the universal law, and driven on, not by ambition, or other unworthy impulse, thou seekest to cast at the feet of men the vast and beautiful efflorescence of thy own mind, shouldst thou find all things around thee conspiring to check and destroy thy imperative development. Thou wilt expand and grow and put forth beauty after beauty; and lo! men will wonder at thee, but seek to destroy thee. Harsh winds will blow their keen arrows into thy face; the crystals of ice will nestle in thy bosom to chill thee unto death; winged demons will probe thee with their stings, and steal away thy perfections. Weep not, and murmur not! It is the law – the law of the star and the flower; of the clod and the nebula. If thou seekest thy own peace and comfort, hide thyself in the caves of the mountains, or the caverns of the ocean; repress all thy longings – check nature in its flight after the ideal; be content to live and not to grow; to exist but not to develop. But canst thou? No, alas! Nature is not to be repressed. Thou, too, must go into the vortices; and in pain and suffering, in mortification and dissolution, pass out to the Unknown!

Nature's Indifference

What then? Well then, imitate Nature in its work, and – its indifference! Keep on never minding. If thou tarriest to pick up the stones flung at thee or to scrape the mud from thy garments, thou wilt never accomplish thy destiny. The energies thou dost waste in fretting or philosophizing about human waywardness or malevolence had better been spent in wholesome work. The time and thought thou expendest in answering the unanswerable, or explaining the inexplicable, would help thee to give the world, out of the storehouse of wholesome thought, new vitalizing principles, fresh forces for well-being and well-doing. Well said the poet: –

Glory of virtue to fight, to struggle, to right the wrong;
Nay, but she aims not a glory, no lover of glory she;
Give her the glory of going on, and for ever to be!

Aye, so it is! Life is for work, not for weeping. Thou, too, hast thy life-work before thee, mapped for thee by the Eternal. It may be the merest drudgery, physical or intellectual; and the results are not be foreseen. Thou must work in the dark, and there is no door outward to the future. But work steadily on! There is thy vocation and redemption: —

Nil actum reputans, si quid superesset agendum!*

Is Gravitation the same Law?

What if some day it were found that this mighty mystery, gravitation, resolved itself into the universal law of expansion and repression? The theory of Le Sage, that the Universe is filled with infinitely minute particles that are continually colliding with larger masses, pushing them forward; but that two large contiguous masses, shielded from the bombardment, are driven irresistibly towards each other, really resolves itself into this. Or, the more recent theory of the vortex atom, whirling around and creating suction in the ether, thus dragging great inert masses toward each other, is not this the same? Why is a column of smoke allowed to ascend and expand into rings or plumes until it is lost in the ether? And why is a column of water from its fountain allowed to expand but a little, and is then thrown back violently on the ground? And why is a stone not allowed to

* Considering nothing done so long as there remains aught to be done.

expand at all, but is flung back peremptorily to the earth? Is it gravitation, or the law of expansion, that obtains fully in the case of smoke, partially in that of water, not at all in the solid matter, unless, as in the case of meteors, the propulsion is so great that is overcomes the resisting and repelling forces, and following its natural or rather the universal tendency, expands into flame, thence into vapor, and is lost? And what a parallel with the meteoric flame of genius!

Schelling

I think Schelling, that most poetical of German philosophers, pushes this idea too far. He makes the usual mistake of poets, of passing from the abstract to the concrete, and lowers a great idea by making it subservient to a whim. One can understand his theory of Creation as being the attempt of the Infinite to embody itself, or rather to expand its supreme energies in the Finite; and also his conception of Mind as the second movement of the universal law by which the Finite, driven back and seeking absorption in the Infinite, unfolds itself in Mind. A Catholic philosopher might seize the idea to illustrate the existence of the Trinity, as the eternal expansion of the Divine Intellect in the contemplation of its own perfections in the World, and the continuous expansion of the Father and Word in the procession of the Spirit from both. When Schelling, driving his theory to extremes, explains the fall of Adam by the tendency to fall away from law and expand into individualism, and the Incarnation as the reunion or contraction of the vagrant human will into the Divine, one cannot help feeling that truth is being distorted into ingenuity, and that freedom is sacrificed at the shrine of 'universal and imperative law.'

15

Is it not singular how that idea of the soul's emanation from God, and its subsequent absorption in God, has always haunted the human mind with its splendid suggestion of a divine origin and a divine destiny? I could never understand how Novalis could call Spinoza a 'god-intoxicated man,' for the latter eliminated God from the Universe, making Him a mere substance, if universal. Schelling would have better earned the description, for he preached at first God as the eternal, self-existent, omniscient, and creative mind. But in very truth the epithet might be applied to every mystic, for all have seemed to be so filled with the idea of the great Supreme Being as to lose themselves in the contemplation, and to have passed into that sublime trance where they have leaped beyond the finite conditions of time and space, and to have touched that which is known as the Absolute. This is the *Potenz der Subsumption* of Schelling; the 'uncreated deep' of Tauler calling to the created, and both becoming one; it is what Denis the Carthusian calls 'the plunging in and the swallowing up of the soul in the Abysm of Divinity;' what Richard of St. Victor calls 'the passing of the soul into God;' what Cardinal Bona describes when he says: 'Thou art I and mine; my whole essence is in Thee.' Somehow it has always seemed to me that, with this strange tendency towards Catholic truth manifested by the wandering intellects of philosophy, some day there will be a reconciliation; or rather these cometary lights, which also have derived whatever is luminous in them from the great uncreated Light of Lights, will be drawn into their right orbits in that mighty system of which Christ is the Eternal Sun. For, whatever far spaces they have illumined, they manifest the tendency of an invincible attraction towards Him. Whilst they wander afar some unseen power seems to draw them towards itself, and to keep them from being lost in space; their light, though they believe themselves self-luminous, is an emanation of the light of the Gospel; and it is the *candor lucis aeternae* that fills their extinguished lamps. How eternally true is the apothegm: *Veram philosophiam esse veram religionem, conversimque veram religionem esse veram philosophiam.**

Is Evolution also Expansion?

And yet an ingenious thinker could construct a theory of the Universe out of this simple law. For what is evolution but a new name for expansion? And the interchange of species; and the systole and diastole of human history; and the expansion of kingdoms and their destruction; and the processes of suns; and the revolutions of seasons; and the eternal strivings of the just and perfect ones; and the aggressions of the wicked; and the growth of genius, and all the many other changes and vicissitudes by which God conserves the equilibrium of His Universe – what are all these secret yet unerring forces but modifications of the universal law: increase and multiply, and – pass? Or, rather, expand, contract, and return?

The Law in Life

There never yet was a Moses without a Miriam, a Socrates without a Xanthippe, a Cæsar without a

---

* True philosophy is true religion, and, conversely, true religion is true philosophy.

Cassius, a Napoleon without his Moscow. The law is universal and inexorable. Every expansive power in Nature and Man, in history, in philosophy, in poetry, has its enemy. Kingdoms do not crumble to pieces from within. It is the outer enemy that destroys. Babylon fell through Cyrus; Jerusalem through Titus; Rome through Vandal and Visigoth; the Eastern Empire through Mohammed; and if moribund kingdoms, like Spain, drag on their lifeless existence through centuries, it is simply because the antagonist has never arisen to attack and destroy. Similarly, every government has its opposition; every statesman, his opponent; every orator, his rival; every poet, his critic. Milton had to fight for his existence; Wordsworth struggled for fifty years for recognition, reluctantly yielded at last; Shelley was hounded from England, and unrecognized for half a century after death; Gifford, the ex-cobbler, and Terry, the actor, drove Keats to a premature grave; and so on with all the brilliant and expansive geniuses of the earth. The tendency of the great is to grow; of the vile, to repress and destroy. God's prerogative of creation and development belongs to the former; man's peculiar bent toward corruption to the latter.

The Law in the Church

Hence, no one need be, or ought to be, surprised at what some call the slow expansion of the Church. She has all the elements of development centered in her strong heart, or tugging at her breasts for that spiritual and intellectual pabulum which will enable them to grow, and vitalize in turn all the torpid faculties of a worn-out, effete civilization. 'Lengthen thy cords, and strengthen thy stakes,' said the Prophet, 'for many are the children of the deserted, rather than of her who hath a husband.' Yet her progress has been slow; and her vast utilities circumscribed. Where she has gained, she has lost; and where she appears the loser, she gains the more. For the first three hundred years of her existence, every attempt to break her bounds, and go forth on her mighty mission, was stopped by fire and sword. When she rose above persecution from without, she was checked by rebellion from within; and her whole history has been a conflict between her own innate and immense potencies and desires for expansion and development, and the outer forces which make for destruction. What she has gained in the New World she has lost in the Old, and *vice versa;* where she has won victories over kings, she has been dishonoured by peoples; what she has gained in art, she has lost in science; and her very hand-maiden, Philosophy, has grown to be her rival in the affections of her children. Yet, still she pursues her immortal destiny, slowly gaining ground over humanity, every check developing her latent strength, every aggression met with indomitable valour; the mustard-seed growing, growing, in spite of wind and weather, the axe and the fire, the Titan and the pigmy, the parasite and the insect, until it fulfils its promised and prophetic destiny, and overshadows all the earth.

The Church in England

In a limited and sectional way, the case of the Church's growth and check in England is conspicuous. Fifty years ago, forces were let loose in that country which promised to extend the spiritual power and supremacy of Catholicism over all the land. The revival in Oxford and elsewhere seemed to promise a universal resurrection. The best moral and intellectual forces in England declared for Rome. So sudden, so important, so frequent were the conversions, that it was fondly hoped that the end of the century would see this ancient Catholic land once more in union with Christendom. Alas! the expansion was but temporary. It was tolerated, only to be driven back with greater force. The united energies of agnosticism, indifferentism, and open infidelity amongst the highest and lowest classes, and the fierce bigotry and intolerance of the dissenting middle classes, not only stemmed, but drove back the tide of intellectual and religious thought which was tending towards Rome. The mighty fissure which the Tractarian Movement made in the Church of England, and which divided its members into the two broad sections of super-naturalism and latitudinarianism was again closed up in a kind of common indifferentism. The time was not opportune. When education is more advanced, and toleration universal, there will be a general movement towards positive religion; and then the final reaction to Catholicism.

The Warden of The Universe

I sat in my garden a few evenings ago. It was in the late summer. The swallows, that had been screaming and circling round and round in evernarrowing rings far up in the clear sky, had gone down to the eaves of my house, where, in their little mud-cabins, they now slept with their young. There was deep silence on all things – silence of midnight, or midseas. A few tendrils of white jasmine had stolen in over my neighbour's wall. The twilight had suddenly departed, and night had come down. I could barely see the white stars of the jasmine, but I could feel their gentle, perfumed breath. Once or twice a vagrant and wanton breeze stole over the wall and seized the top tassels of my Austrian pine, and lifted the sleepy leaves of the sycamores, which murmured and fell back to rest. Then silence again, deep as the grave! I saw the suns of space, glinting green and red and yellow. I felt the throb of the Universe. As the lookout on a great steamer on the high seas, staring into the darkness, feels the mighty vessel throb beneath him, and watches the phosphorescence of the waves, and hears the beat of the engines, so felt I the thrill of Being – the vibration of existence. And, as far up in the darkness on the bridge of the vessel, silent, invisible, stands the captain, who controls the mighty mechanism beneath him – dumb, watchful, with a light touch on the electric knob before him, so I saw Thee, though Thou, too, wert invisible, O my God – I saw Thy finger on the magnetic key of Thy Universe; and I feared not the night, nor the darkness, nor the grave, for I knew that the destinies of us and of Thy worlds were safe in Thy keeping.

Science shall never advance on right lines, except by imitating God. It is the wisdom of God in its infancy!

Finite and Infinite

I love the science that reveals. I hate the science that explains, or affects to explain. I confess I revel in mysteries. The more profound and cryptic they are, the greater is my faith and delight. The merely natural palls on me. I see, wonder, measure, and – despise. I feel that I am its equal, no matter how stupendous it is. I measure myself with it, and lo! I am head and shoulders over it. The tiny retina of the eye of a child clasps the whole dome of worlds. The soul of a hind grasps the revealed universe, whilst he wonders at it. But the mightiest telescope ever invented and the all-searching eye of science cannot penetrate the impenetrable, the Universal; and the mind of a Newton or a Leibniz sinks paralyzed by Infinity. Tell me all the 'fairy tales of Science.' I wonder and am glad. But in a little time the wonder ceases. Weigh your suns and analyze them! Calculate your distances by billions and trillions of miles! Reveal your purple stars, and the radiant light that is flung from two or three varicoloured suns upon their happy planets. I thank you for the revelation. I exult and am glad. But don't go one step further! Don't speak of Impersonal Force or Universal Motion as explanatory of such mystery! This time again I laugh, not in pleasure, but in scorn, or rather pity.

The Supernatural

People say to me: 'Never seen Rome! or Florence! St. Peter's! the frescoes of the Sistine! The galleries in the Pitti Palace!' Not yet. But if I were to go to Italy I would go to see the Supernatural, because it is the only thing I could really and permanently admire. I would go to Rome, and see the Spiritual Head of Christ's Empire; I would go to Loreto, and kiss the ground once trodden by Jesus and Holy Mary. I would go to Assisi; and walk every step of the *Via Crucis* the 'poor man' trod. I would make a pilgrimage to Siena; and I would visit every *stigmatica* and *ecstatica*. And there in her humble chamber, I would wonder and rejoice! I would have emotions which the grandeur of St. Peter's, and the terrors of Vesuvius, and the beauties of Naples, and the sublimity of Pompeii could never excite. For I would come into touch with the Supernatural – with God; and the work of His fingers is more to me than the most stupendous creations of human hands.

Knowledge and Reverence

It is a good thing for men to be scientific. It makes them so humble. At least, it ought to make them so. I am quite prepared to hear that St. Thomas and Suarez were the humblest of men; that Newton and Leibniz were little children. It is only right and reasonable. When the former in their tremendous researches into some awful mystery, like the Trinity, evolved proposition after proposition, unwound, as it were, the cerements of the awful secret, and then laid down their pens, like the scribes of old, and covered their faces, and murmured with full hearts: Sanctus! Sanctus! Sanctus! one can admire them whilst pitying them. But when a sciolist, also, unwrapping mystery after mystery, in search of the Great First Cause, comes suddenly upon an adamantine secret, that refuses to be broken or unweft, and lays down his pen and mutters, Unknowable! one can pity and despise!

The Secret Cabinets of God

God is quite right. He keeps locked the secret chambers of His knowledge and His works, because He knows that if He opened them, we would despise Him. Leibniz said, that if he had a choice, he would prefer the pursuit of knowledge forever to the sudden acquisition of perfect knowledge. One of the many pleasures of heaven will be the eternal, but slow unlocking of the secret cabinets of God. There must be mysteries, or man's pride would equal Lucifer's. It is God's way from the beginning. 'Of all the trees of the garden, thou may'st eat; but of this one thou shalt not eat!' No one shall enter the Holy of Holies but the High Priest; and that but once a year! No wonder they tied a rope to his sacrificial vestments to drag forth his dead body, if Jehovah smote him. And yet the Lord is not in the thunder and the storm, but in the breathing of zephyrs, and the sighs of the gentle breeze!

Intuition

To a certain class of mind the doctrine of our intuitive knowledge of God has a peculiar fascination. It seems so much higher and more honourable than the slow acquisition of ideas through the senses, that I am quite sure it would give unbounded gratification to this school of Catholic idealists, if it could be shown that it was not inconsistent with the most approved scheme of Catholic philosophy. Some writers deem it quite untenable, as tending to Ontologism. But it may happen that in this, as in so many other things, the confusion arises in tongues, – in different meanings and interpretations of the same word. That fine thinker and metaphysician, Father Dalgairns,* seems to teach in his standard work on *The Holy Communion,* that the idea of God is inborn and immediately certain; that the Fathers call man, θεοδίδακτος; that man holds in himself the seeds of the knowledge of God (τὰ σπέρματα τῆς θεογνωσίας;) and all this chimes in so harmoniously with all the expe-

* Quoting Hettinger. Appendix D. *Holy Communion: et passim.*

24

riences and feelings of the above-named school, that it would be an incalculable pleasure and delight to them to know that they might hold such beautiful and transcendent truths, and yet be at one with the great scholastics, and the most approved views of modern philosophy. There are few souls whom the lines of Wordsworth do not haunt as if with the revelation of a spirit-world: –

> And I have felt
> A presence that disturbs me with the joy
> Of elevated thoughts; a sense sublime
> Of something far more deeply interfused,
> Whose dwelling is the light of setting suns,
> And the round ocean and the living air,
> And the blue sky, and in the mind of man;
> A motion and a spirit that impels
> All thinking things, all objects of all thought;
> And rolls through all things.

Man's Intuition. God's Revelation

This ethereal sense, this quick intuitive perception, which has so often thrown back upon themselves the finest souls, and moved them by its swift and sudden revelation of the infinite even to tears, is something altogether apart from mere logic or reason. Nay, perhaps, we had best interpret it as not so much a momentary penetration of the spirit behind the veils, as the sudden break in the clouds that hide God's Face; and the swift dawning, clouded in a moment again, of that transcendent Light that makes the heaven of heavens luminous by its splendours. Hence let us say that this swift perception of the Infinite is not so much the effort of unrestrained fancy, or imagination, as the sudden revelation of God to

25

choice spirits, – the swift and unexpected rending of the veil, the parting of the cloud for a moment; and then, the darkness, but no longer the doubt. This is akin to the condition ἔνθεος καὶ ἔκφρων 'bereft of reason, but filled with God'; the sense of the vision,

> when the light of sense
> Goes out, but with a flash that has revealed
> The invisible world.

Intuition in the Schools

This intuitional principle of knowledge, although attributed in its origin to the pantheistic school of Schelling, is really the property of all poetical minds. In the German school it passed to the extreme of subjective Pantheism, just as in the Neo-Platonic schools it became a most dangerous form of mysticism. But that it is not irreconcilable with more prosaic forms of thought may be shown by the not incurious fact that the Scottish school of philosophy, essentially and professedly the school of common sense, is also the great school where the intuitional perception of God is unreservedly taught. The Scottish universities have, particularly of recent years, returned to the Aristotelian method, and with it to the intuitional philosophy. Reid, Brown, and, greatest of all, Hamilton, have been ardent Aristotelians. The latter presented the Organon, the Nichomachean Ethics, and the Rhetoric of Aristotle to the Oxford Examiners when about to be examined for his degree; and it is said of him that he took up the first great treatise as a recreation when wearied of kindred studies, so completely had he mastered it and so easy had its abstruse metaphysics become. Yet he lays his greatest claim to fame to the fact that he first affected to have bridged over the chasm that yawned between mind and substance; and his disciples maintain that this was his original contribution to modern thought. What was his secret, what the airy bridge that he flung from the solid basework of consciousness across the dark and unspanned gulf that cut away that consciousness from the external world? How did he pass from consciousness of the Idea to consciousness of the Represented? By intuition! It may or may not be accepted as the final solution of the one great problem of metaphysics, and many will be disposed to think it leaves matters just as they were. Nevertheless it is significant that a mind so strongly rationalistic should seek in intuition the key of the great arcanum, and yet cling to the rigid precision of the great mediæval schools. And this tradition, left by Scotland's greatest thinker, has passed down into and been incorporated with the teaching of the great universities, until the present professor in the chair of philosophy at St. Andrew's rejects every other argument for the existence of God – cosmological, teleological, etc. – and pins all his faith to the intuitional method. And then, perhaps, if all were known, it would be found that the intuition of philosophers, no matter how veiled in the strange terminology of the science, is, after all, something akin to Faith.

Wordsworth

Strange, too, is it that all modern agnostics seem to claim Wordsworth as their prophet. His vague abstractions supply the place of religion, without binding the mind to dogma. It is the concrete, the defined, against which the pride of intellect persistently revolts. It will not say *Credo!* but *Sentio!* It puts the Absolute, the Unconditioned, the Non-Ego, the soul of Nature, in place of 'God, the Father Almighty, Creator of Heaven and Earth.' It puts agnosticism in place of limitation, incognizable for incomprehensible. It declares the mystery of the Universe insoluble, because the only possible solution implicates them in a declaration of faith. But man's soul must have something to believe in, even if it were a devil. But that 'something' must not limit human freedom, nor arrogate rights over humanity, nor disturb liberty of action and thought, and, above all, it must not be the Arbiter and Judge of the Living and the Dead. But God is all that in the Christian hegemony. Well, then, they say, we must fall back upon the Impersonal, the Uncreated, the Soul of things.

The Secret of his Influence

We shall worship in 'temples not made of hands;' our liturgy shall be poetry; our ritual, the changes of the seasons; our sacrament, communion with Nature; our priesthood, the poet or the philosopher; and our apotheosis, the general absorption of all that we are or shall be into the universal Soul! No wonder that Wordsworth, who wrote so bitterly against the Church, as the 'enemy of all mental and moral freedom,' should be the High Priest of the new dispensation. I think this is really the secret of his power over moderns. It is not his poetry, which is but a purple patch here and there on his gaberdine; nor his philosophy, which is bald and bare enough; but this communion with Nature and worship of it, and tacit exclusion of the supernatural in the Christian sense, that makes him popular with such writers as Matthew Arnold, or Mrs. Humphrey Ward, or

Emerson. He is not a pantheist; such a term is quite inapplicable to Wordsworth. He is a Pythagorean, admitting at the same time, but concealing, the existence of the Supreme Being, and concentrating all his thoughts on the *Anima Mundi*.

Not a Pantheist

And yet, though I have quoted Wordsworth here as an example of the Intuitionist, I feel that I am somewhat in error. He has been quoted as an apologist for Pantheism; as a defender of Christian Theism. His friends do not seek to refute the former aspersion; his enemies are careless about the latter imputation. Yet, he is neither one nor the other. It is not the God of Spinoza he beholds and hears, for Spinoza saw nothing but dumb, irresponsive matter with its one essential of extension; neither does he address that personal God, whom we know as distinct from His universe, yet permeating it,

Intra cuncta, nec inclusus,
Extra cuncta, nec exclusus.*

His appeal is to the 'Presences of Nature in the Sky,' 'The Visions of the Hills,' 'The Souls of Lonely Places,' the

... sentiment of Being spread
O'er all that moves, and all that seemeth still;
'The Eternal Soul, clothed in the brook, with purer
robes than those of flesh and blood.'

* Within all things, but not included
  Outside all things, but not excluded.

But all this is not the delirium of Pantheism, even in the diluted shape, called 'Higher Pantheism,' nor yet is it the quiet worship of God, the Creator and Consecrator. It is simply the instinct, or faculty, of Personification; the creation from his own poetic subjectivity of the *Anima Mundi,* – the soul that belongs to all inferior creation; the response to the beauty and mystery and symbolism of the earth. And it is strange that the poet, who possessed this sensibility to a far higher degree than Wordsworth, and whose writings are one extended personification, of all the powers, passions and sympathies of Nature, is never quoted either as a Pantheist, or as a Deist. Yet he is the poet of abstractions and idealism; and he has written more poetry than Wordsworth has written prose. And this is a momentous word.

The Poet, a Creator

This faculty of personification of the abstract – of casting the features of one's own mind across landscape, or human passion, or human history, is really what has given such reflective intellects a right to the title – Poet. That dogmatic and rather haughty saying of Tasso:

Non cè in mundo chi merita nome di Creatore, che Dio ed il Poeta, *

has some foundation in reason. Other artists work on rude materials, and fashion and form them according to their concepts. The poet creates his own materials, makes his own divinities, and worships them. In a kind of Bacchic fury he calls up visions from the vasty deep,

* No one deserves the name of Creator, but God and the Poet.

and blows them back into nothingness again. He is the necromancer of Nature – that is, when he is a real poet, not a mere scene painter for the greater dramatist, Nature. Hence, too, is he priest and prophet, uttering sometimes in an unknown language, the secrets of high and hidden things; and each poet has his own neophytes and disciples, who study his language, imitate his style, try to find not only the symmetry, but the symbolism of his words, and sit at his feet in life, at the foot of his statue when dead, and call him their master, their teacher, and their king.

Shelley

And yet, strange to say, one of the greatest of these creators founds an argument for the non-existence of God in the formula: Mind can only perceive, it can never create; adding, however, the saving clause, 'so far as we know Mind.' Quite so! But man's mind is the lowest spirituality. And to argue from that to the powers of the Supreme and Sovereign Mind, is a strange fatuity. But is it true that man's mind does not create? Where, then, O Poet of Atheism, was your Alastor, and your Beatrice, and your Prometheus, before you created them; where the 'Eve of this Eden,' the 'ruling grace of the sweet garden'; where the 'Desires and Adorations,' 'winged Persuasions and veiled Destinies' that wept over Adonais; where

The legion of wild thoughts, whose wandering wings
Now float above thy darkness, and now rest
Where that and thou art no unbidden guest
In the still cave of the witch, poesy?

Either there is no poet, but only a scene-painter, either

there is no poetry, but word-painting; or else there is a projection over nature and man of a something which is not theirs.

'A light that never was on sea or land;' and a strange reflection, where hover all beautiful forms of the Imagination, are not merely what the poet perceives or imagines, but the distinct creation of his mind.

Idealism

Some one, I am almost sure it is Emerson, has said that every great thinker must be, at one time or another in his life, an Idealist. Idealism is the land of dreams and visions, into which every new, fine spirit passes and wanders, dazed and blind, not knowing what to think, and rather inclined to believe that life and all its surroundings is a delusion – some vision painted by a sprite of evil, to torture or distress, or madden him with its beauteous unrealities. Then, one day, he leaps over the bridge of Common Sense and Experience, and finds himself in the world of hard and stern realities. He rubs his eyes, and wonders was he dreaming; touches and handles things without being able to prove their substance. Then reverts very often into his dream again, and murmurs this musical monologue:

We look on that which cannot change – the One,
The unborn and the undying. Earth and Ocean,
Space, and the isles of life and light that gem
The sapphire floods of interstellar air,
This firmament pavilioned upon chaos,
With all its cressets of immortal fire,
Whose outwall, bastioned impregnably
Against the escape of boldest thoughts, repels them
As Calpe the Atlantic clouds – this Whole

Of suns, and worlds, and men, and beasts and flowers,
With all the silent or tempestuous workings
By which they have been, are, or cease to be,
Is but a vision; all that it inherits
Are motes of a sick eye, bubbles and dreams;
Thought is its cradle and its grave, nor less
The future and the past are idle shadows,
Of thought's eternal flight – they have no being;
Nought is but that which feels itself to be.

Pre-existence

Recent researches in physiology throw considerable light
on that favourite doctrine, or rather speculation, of
poets and philosophers, *Pre-existence*. It has haunted the
imagination of men from the beginning of the world; and
shaped itself in all kinds of worthy and degrading
assumptions. Like all other forms of mysticism, it had
its cradle in the East; thence it shadowed itself on the
great mind of Plato, under the form of *anamnesis,* or
memory of former existence; and in this shape it has
become familiar to us through Shelley, who was a
professed Platonist, and in the remarkable lines of
Wordsworth, in his *Intimations of Immortality:* –

Our birth is but a sleep and a forgetting;
The soul that rises with us, our life's Star,
Hath had elsewhere its setting,
And cometh from afar.
Not in entire forgetfulness,
And not in utter nakedness,
But trailing clouds of glory do we come
From God, who is our home.

But such hauntings as of a former existence are not limited
to poets, whose minds are supersensitive to impressions.

There are few persons, and these of dull metal, who are not sometimes startled by the vivid reminiscences which arise on visiting some strange place, which certainly they had never seen before. This feeling differs altogether from the sudden flashes of memory that are struck from hearing some old, familiar, but forgotten strain of music; or from the sudden fragrance of a flower, or the grouping of clouds at sunset, or the ashen light of an October afternoon.

It is a sudden sensation that some time in our lives we have been here, seen those objects, just as now they are pictured to our waking vision. Nor is it the shadow cast by the vanishing skirts of a dream, vivid in its intensity, and which the waking brain fails to cast aside under the more imperious calls of reality. But there it is; and we have been here before. How can we explain it? By the theory of double consciousness, and the unequal action, therefore the unequal sensitiveness of the two great factors, or lobes in the brain. We know now that these lobes can act quite independently of each other; that one can display the greatest activity, whilst the other is torpid; and that often, particularly under the pressure of necessity, the torpid, dormant lobe takes up its duties and emulates in its sensitiveness its more active brother. If we suppose, then, a person whose cerebral power is functionally impaired by the imperfect interaction of the two lobes of the brain, coming suddenly upon a perfectly strange scene, the first impression made upon the healthy-active lobe will be of perfect strangeness and unfamiliarity. But in a short time the other lobe wakes up to active consciousness; and the impressions made by the first are cast upon it, thus creating a reminiscence as of something once and long ago experienced or seen. Alas! that science should be so ruthless; even though it has the honour of accommodating itself to scholastic and strictly logical reasoning. It is not the only case where the conclusions of science are at one with the venerable traditions of the Church.

SECTION II.

Plato and Aristotle

This chain of thought which connects the conclusions of science with the traditions of the Church drags in another link out of the deep seas of speculation – the respective influences of Plato and Aristotle on the Scholastic teaching of the Church. There can hardly be a doubt that the former did hold sway through all the earlier centuries of the Church's existence, in the famous schools at Alexandria, along the Pontine shore, at Constantinople, and the cities of the Euxine Sea, until at last, after colouring with its poetry all the theology, philosophy and oratory of the East, it finally degenerated into the mysticism of the Neo-Platonists; and Rome, ever watchful of the truth, had to step in, and check the degeneration by recalling men's minds to fact and doctrine and away from dream and speculation. Yet it always haunted the East with its poetic splendours, until the tremendous reaction of mediæval times towards the Aristotelian method of reasoning drove Platonism back into the shades of history and tradition. And from these mediæval times downwards, the Aristotelian philosophy, with its contempt for poetry, its hard, dry analysis, and the rigid formalism of the syllogism, has been accepted informally as the philosophic *method* of the Church. The *Summa* of St. Thomas, the impregnable bulwark of Catholic philosophic teaching, is founded on it. The spirit of the Stagyrite passed into the 'dumb Sicilian ox,' and through his mouth spoke to the world.

The Aristotelian Method

There cannot, too, be the slightest doubt that, if the mission of the Catholic Church on earth be to teach truth, and guard the Divine Revelation, this is in reality the most effective and, we might say, Divinely-ordained means of doing so. There must be no question of poetry, rhetoric, or sophistry here. The graces of human eloquence, the lofty flights of poetry, the garlands and the flowers of human fancy, have their own place; but they have no place here. Truth is naked: the Clothes-Philosophy, which has always dominated the ideas of men, has nothing to say to the naked majesty of this heaven-sprung deity. So far, then, as the preservation or exposition of Truth goes, it is clear it must be couched in the strictest terminology; and doctrine must be defined with as close a logical accuracy as human language, as expressive of human ideas, will permit. Therefore, the syllogism and the definition are the only rhetorical embellishments theology, in its official form, can permit. Hence, for six hundred years the Aristotelian method has prevailed in the schools of the Church. And it has been justified in its adoption by the fact that the moment the human mind broke away from it in that first disastrous Enthymeme of Descartes: *Cogito, ergo sum,* it drifted further and further away in the endless mazes of human speculation, until at last it completely lost itself in the visionary ideas of the German Pantheists, or the still worse, because more contemptuous, dogmatism of French Encyclopædists. In our own days, the world, emerging from the horrid labyrinths of rationalism and infidelity, is rubbing its darkened eyes; and still blinded by the darkness, is only able as yet to declare in a dazed and despairful way:

Behold, we know not anything!

What the World Wants

But now the question arises, whether in view of the world's awakening to the proximate and insistent issues that lie before it, it may not be well to reconsider our position; and, bearing in mind the strong prejudices that still exist against Scholasticism, try to present our truths not as dry bones, but as clothed and living realities. This suggestion, of course, only applies to our presentation of truth to the world. In our own colleges, there can be no great change from the rigid, logical method, because such method is preparatory and fundamental, and, therefore, strictly formal. But it is almost certain that we are on the eve of a tremendous reaction from agnosticism and materialism; and consequently from the inductive system of logic that led mankind into the abyss. That reaction will not take place on logical lines of thought. The world is too tired of analysis to care for more. It will clamour for the poetic, for the ideal. We must do for it what the Greek Fathers and St. Augustine did for the peoples who were waking out of the horrible dreams of heathenism. For men not only reason, but feel. The higher aspirations must be fed, as well as the ratiocinative faculties. Mere logic never made a saint; nor mere reasoning a convert.

Plato

Frederick Schlegel, I believe, says that every man is born a Platonist, or an Aristotelian. There is food enough for the latter. Why should the former be starved? Goethe interprets the idea expressed in Raffaelle's famous picture of the school of Athens, where Aristotle is represented with his face bent to the earth, whereas Plato looks up to Heaven, thus: 'Plato's relation to the world is that of a superior spirit, whose good pleasure it is to dwell in it for a time. He penetrates their depths, more that he may replenish them from the fulness of his own nature, than that he may fathom their mysteries.' It is quite true his doctrines of emanation, pre-existence, and innate ideas cannot now be held by a child of the Church; but he so far foreshadowed the cardinal doctrines of Christianity that it is not difficult to accept the tradition that he sat at the feet of the prophet Jeremias in India; impossible to disbelieve that the whole of the Jewish or rather Judaic theology was known to him. The existence of the Word, a triune Divinity, the nothingness of life, the immortality of the soul, the rejection of Deities, the acceptance of Monotheism, the refutation of Atheism, the existence of great principles and eternal laws of right or wrong, as apart from utilitarian ideas of happiness or comfort – all these he taught with the emphasis of a Doctor of the Church. And he seems to have refuted the agnosticism of his own day by his constant appeal to the demonstrations and axioms of geometry as certainties that can be known. His most modern admirer, Dr. Whewell, puts his case strongly:

It was these truths which really gave origin to sound philosophy, by exhibiting examples of *certain* truths. They refuted the scepticism which had begun to cry out, *Nothing can be known*, by saying in a manner which men could not deny, *This can be known!* In like manner they may refute the scepticism which says, *We can know nothing of God*, by saying *We know this of God, that necessary truths are true to Him.*

Alas for Plato! and alas for Dr. Whewell! Down come John Stuart Mill and Sir John Herschell, and affect to shatter the theory of Necessary Truths to atoms! And so the fabric of Philosophy is Tennyson's fabled city,

...built to music,
And therefore never built at all,
And therefore built forever.

His Influence

There can be no doubt that whatever be said of his philosophy, he has exercised a wider and deeper influence on human thought than any other seer of ancient or modern times. He was regarded as an apostle by the early Fathers. Justin Matyr, Jerome, and Lactantius speak of him as the greatest of philosophers. Augustine traces half his conversion to him. The whole Eastern Church, especially the Church of Clement and Origen at Alexandria, held him in deepest reverence. Amongst modern thinkers, Emerson traces his direct influence in Boethius, Erasmus, Locke, Alfieri, Coleridge, Copernicus, Newton, Goethe, Sir Thomas More, Henry More, Lord Bacon, Jeremy Taylor, etc., besides the host of minor philosophers and major poets who have taken their inspiration from him. Dante, whilst praising Aristotle as the 'Master of those who know,' borrows largely and without acknowledgment from Plato; for what is his famous vision of the 'singing suns': –

> Io vidi più fulgor vivi e vincenti
>> Far di noi centro e di sè far corona,
>> Più dolci in voce che in vista lucenti.

> Poi, si cantando, quegli ardenti soli
>> Si fur girati intorno a noi tre volte,
>> Come stelle vicine ai fermi poli.
> *Paradiso*, Canto X., 64-76.*

* Then saw I many a glow, living and conquering,

but the 'wheel with eight vast circles of divers colours, and in the circles eight stars fixed; and, as the spindle moved they moved with it; and in each circle a syren stood, singing in one note, and thus from the eight stars arose one great harmony of sound.'**

Platonism and Neo-Platonism

Nor should it be forgotten that is was Averroës, the first of the European pantheists, that introduced the Aristotelian system into Europe; that if Plotinus, Iamblichus, Porphyry, and Proclus were fanatics and dangerous ones, Plutarch and Boethius were also Platonists; that many commentators in more recent times regard the Platonic doctrines of emanation, pre-existence and planetary souls as poetic conceptions, not doctrinal teachings, for Plato, though he despised poets like Homer, and would give them no place in his *Republic,* was essentially a poet himself and of a high order; and it must not also be forgotten that it was Descartes, now regarded as the parent of all modern agnosticism, who gave the death-blow to Realism, and established that Nominalism, of which Hobbes, Locke, Berkeley and Hume were subsequent exponents. The truth is that Platonism has got an evil reputation from the excesses of its interpreters, especially the Neo-Platonists. Yet it is at least doubtful whether the Mysticism into which they dragged the

Make of us centre, and of themselves a crown,
Sweeter of voice than shining in appearance

When, so singing, those burning suns
   Had circled around us thrice,
   Like stars neighbouring the fixed poles.
** *Republic,* Book X.

doctrines of their Master was not a less dangerous form of heresy than that world-wide materialism, with which we have to contend, and of which Plato was, and is, the most successful antagonist.

Philosophy and Literature

But the truth appears to be that Platonism, which has an evil sound, owing to the excesses of its followers and commentators, has had at all times a great influence in the formation of thought. St. Thomas made Dante a philosopher; but Plato made Dante a poet. But, setting aside the names of founders of systems, and regarding only the development of doctrine, it would seem an opportune time to place before the world what some would call the transcendental, others the ethico-intellectual side of Catholicity. And whilst St. Thomas' *Summa* reigns supreme in the schools as the *system* of sound philosophy, there can be no reason why St. Augustine and the Greek Fathers in theology; Dante and Calderon in poetry; the Schlegels in literature; St. Teresa, St. John of the Cross, St. Francis of Assisi in ascetic science; and such moderns as Balmez, Dalgairns, Faber, Gratry, etc., in popularized philosophy, should not be put forward to represent the more attractive phases of Christian science. The poorer classes have our churches and music; the artists our galleries, and all the poetry of our faith frozen in eternal marble, or frescoed in everlasting colours; musicians have all the divine delights of Mozart, Handel, Haydn, in Masses and Oratories; but τίς φωνεῖ συνέτοις in modern language and with modern adaptations? The student who, some day, will take down Suarez's *Metaphysics* and give it to the world in strong, resonant, rhythmical English, will be one of the intellectual leaders of his generation.

God holds in His hands the balance of the Universe. The Church on earth holds the balance of truth. The equilibrium of the former is disturbed by a feather's weight; that of the latter by a word, a syllable, a vowel. I cast a stone into the sea, and its fall is felt on far and unknown shores. I utter one word; it touches for good or evil souls as yet unborn or unconceived. There appears to be but a hair's breadth of difference between the *sensism* of Locke and St. Thomas' theory of the Origin of Ideas. The hair's breadth swells to the yawning chasm of Truth and Un-Truth. The ravings of a Neo-Platonist and the mysticism of St. Teresa and St. John of the Cross seem the same. They are as far apart as the poles. And between that sense of the Infinite, the realization of God's Presence, the light touch of His hand, the breathing of the Spirit, the parting in the cloud, and the *Intellectual Intuition* of Schelling, by which reason knows the Absolute, because itself is the Absolute, and the Absolute can only exist as known by reason; how slender the verbal difference, how wide apart the faith and common sense of the one from the philosophical delirium of the other! And how necessary that infallible *magisterium* that is forever checking the turbulent and riotous waves of thought with its imperious command: 'Thus far shalt thou come, and no farther.'

Soul and Body

It is Vico who says:

God is to the world what the soul is to the body.

As an analogy or comparison, Yes! As a fact, No! You cannot call God the *Anima Mundi* or the *Forma Mundi*. But you can mount up from the consciousness of the *Ego* and its powers, and even its limitations, by a strict, severe analogy, to the idea of God; the Finite cannot evolve the Infinite, but it suggests it. And granted the immateriality of the soul, you leap at once to the idea of the Infinite Mind – God. *Cogito, ergo sum!* said the soldier-philosopher. *Cogito, et volo, ergo sum supra cognitionem et volitionem*, says the Christian thinker.

It is quite certain than no organ can command or control itself. The heart, the liver, the lungs, are mostly automatic. They are beyond the power of will in their operations. They work in obedience to a mysterious force, called Life. But the brain is not automatic in its workings. It is controlled from without. By what? The *ego*, the soul, which thinks, acts, operates, controls, subdues, excites, mollifies; or if it fails to do so, it is not so much through lack of will, though the will is weak, but because the instrument is broken or passed beyond control. How marvellous is that power of volition to call up the faculty of memory! An instant, and lo! the great map of the past is unrolled; and there, in indelible ink, is the diorama of our life, or any section of our life. Faces, scenes, works, words, touches, looks, sounds, odours – all gleam out in the clear handwriting of the past; and, as we will, or when the obedient instrument we command is weary, we fold up the map again and put it away, secure that neither time nor trial shall dim their colours, or cause their sweet associations to cease.

Frankenstein's Monster

Frankenstein constructed a monster; but he failed to give him a soul. He gave him brain, intellect, mind; but it remained a mere mechanical toy. It was corporeal, intellectual, sensitive, passionate, swayed by emotions, a prey to terrors, or what is worse than terror, the power to create it. But it was irresponsible. Its greatest crime could not be imputed to it, because it had no soul; and no frame-builder, however skilled of hand, or keen of mind, could ever pretend to give it.

Spiritual Essences

They who deny the existence of spirits deny the reality of other than organic life. Our idea of life is limited to certain organisms, frail and temporary, to some subtle influence that prevents them from falling into an inorganic condition; and which gives them facilities and powers extremely limited in operation, yet with unquenchable aspirations after higher ideals. But, analyze as you will, this life, even in man, is a force, substantial in its immaterial essence though it be. To suppose that this is the only potentiality in the Universe, exercised in this humble and limited way, is nonsense. The same force must be exerted in far higher and loftier ways; therefore in far higher and nobler beings, inorganic and incorporeal, but transcendently intellectual.

Thought is not nerve-tension

The automatic nerves in the spinal cord, motor and sensory, and the sympathetic nerves outside the cord are free from the operations of consciousness, and uncontrolled by them. Why does not volition extend to them, if volition is a mere development of nervous power? Why is it limited to the cerebrum, and inoperative in the rest of the nervous system? If thought is only nerve-tension, and volition the same, why is thought localized in the brain, and even in different convolutions of the brain, although the physiologists have to admit the consensus of all parts of the brain to rational and consecutive thought?

The King in Exile

I notice, too, that depression comes from dyspepsia, or solitude, or grief, or overwork. It is a functional brain-disease. The blood is impure in the capillaries, or some nerve, pneumogastric or other, is irritated, and sets up in the great ganglions irritation and consequent depression. Yet I can control it, and even banish it. By what? The mind. But it is the mind itself that is functionally disordered and made impotent and incapable. Then, by some power beyond the mind and independent of it in existence, if not by action. This is the 'spark and divine potentiality of man,' as the Mystics say: 'The unlost and the inalienable nobleness of man – that from which,' as Pascal says, 'his misery as well as his glory proceeds – that which must ever exist in hell, and be converted into sorrow there.' The King in Exile, warring with rebellious subjects, recalling lost royalties with pain or remorse, yet never abdicating or sacrificing the majesty of his heritage, but ever dreaming of the restoration of his kingdom and his throne – even such is, or should be, the mighty soul in its disenthronement.

The faculty of Attention

If Idealism cannot be accepted as a rational scheme, or explanation, of the phenomena of thought, sensism is still more burdened with difficulties which admit of no explanation. For when you have pursued its operations to their remotest end, you have still the difficulty of *attention* to explain; and a hundred other questions confront you that can only be interpreted by fresh creations of the imagination. In fact, when you have reached the terminus of physiological operations, you cannot go further in your research after the ever-vanishing and elusive mystery of thought, without creating or imagining a soul. I sit here in my garden, talking with a friend. I am absorbed in conversation; but my eyes are fixed not on the face of my companion, but on that flower that burns itself on the retina of my eye, though ten feet away in its bed. Its colour and form inprint themselves after passing through the canal of the eye, on the retina. They touch the optic nerve, and are carried along the electric wire of the nerve, until they reach their term, and paint themselves on the sensorium of the brain. They cannot go further. That operation of vision, physiologically considered, is perfected. The object is imprinted on the brain as clearly as my seal is imprinted on the hot sealing wax. Yet I do not see that flower. I am so absorbed in this conversation with my friend that I no more perceive that tulip than I see the roses of the Gardens of Shiraz.

Its limitation and power

But suddenly, yes, I see it! I see its red and yellow colours and its chalice shape. How? By what new oper-

47

ation? The sensorium of the brain has already been reached, touched, and affected by the image cast from the rays of light which have proceeded from the flower. What new faculty has been brought into operation? Clearly nothing cerebral or even physical. Something has suddenly swooped down upon that material representation, looked at it, studied it, seen it, recognized it. Before that moment of recognition, the image was there as clearly as after its discovery. But it was unseen, unknown, unrecognized. Who is the mysterious discoverer? Who has seen into the tiny caverns of the brain, and studied just at that point of light at the end of the optic nerve that brightly-coloured picture? Another cerebral faculty? Impossible. The cells of the brain are imbedded with their mysterious faculties in their own matrices, nor can they move or be moved, from place to place, by their own automatic power, or by secret energies. Each cell has its own energy, its own faculty, its own operation. It cannot come forth from its setting to gaze at pictures, or hear sounds in other places. Clearly, then, the faculty of attention or observation must be an independent faculty, to move hither and thither upon its mysterious mission. It must be a swift and subtle faculty to pass from sensorium to sensorium with the rapidity of light. It must be an imperious and arbitrary faculty, for there is no disputing its demands, if the instrument is still unbroken. Memory must give up its secrets, and unfold its maps of persons, landscapes, sounds, sensations, pleasures, pains – at its behest. It groups sensations, past, present, and future, together, and forms ideas and principles from their collation. It grasps facts of the external world – takes them from natural history, from human history, from art, from science, and builds up systems, from which in turn it takes principles of guidance – synthesizing, analyzing, weaving, unweaving across the woof of the brain

the webs of fancy or the tapestry of thought; and all
this wonderful and miraculous work is the result of that
secret and celestial mechanism – the cell? No! the
Soul!

Volition the Source of all heroic action

But there is something more. There is a sister faculty,
under that Mother-Soul, whose power is still more sur-
prising. Volition is greater than intellect, for intellect
may stimulate volition, but volition commands intellect.
And if the doctrine of mere sensism cannot account for
thought, still less can it account for that mysterious
faculty which dominates thought and sense equally. If
all movements of thought and will were obedient to
sense, what hogs from the sty of Epicurus would we be!
What room would there be for all those superhuman
deeds that have gilded the otherwise sombre pages of
human history? How would you explain the nobility of
Abraham, as with uplifted knife, and with all the instincts of nature protesting, he sought to immolate his
son at the command of God? Or the courage of a David
facing the maniac Saul? Or the heroism of a Scaevola,
a Brutus, a Cato, a Germanicus? Or the patriotism of
a Hofer or a Tell? And how would you explain the filling
of sandy deserts with converted voluptuaries from
Athens, and Alexandria, and Rome? Or a Stylites on his
lonely pillar, or the unnumbered martyrs who gave up
their lives as witnesses to the Unseen? If sense alone
created thought, or governed will, how will you explain
this revolt against all its arbitrary dictates? Is it not
more reasonable to accept the existence of a superior
faculty, that, strengthened and enlightened from above,
can trample the senses beneath its feet, and compel to

action on far higher and loftier principles than either sense or reason could suggest?

The Imprisoned Soul

But how pitiful is the soul in its imprisonment! How sad to see so noble a creation, with all its tremendous aspirations and possibilities, dependent for its knowledge on the tiny miniatures of external things cast upon one pin-point of the cerebral substance; and on the other hand, eternally fretted by the rebellion of those very senses which are its ministers and slaves. Now and again, in moments of inspiration, it seems to emancipate itself from these trammels of the flesh and to soar out and beyond its prison. Saints have experienced this in their ecstasies, poets in their dreams. It comes to some souls in the flush of early morning with the songs of newly awakened birds, and the smell of wet woods; and it comes at eventide with the saffron skies, and the slow death of day. It is at these times that the soul it not so much lifted up towards God, as driven to drag down heaven and God to earth. It seems to fling its arms around Infinity and to embrace it, and be lost in it. The rapture lasts but for one moment, whilst the soul feels unutterable things. Then once more it sinks back into its prison, and drags after it the heavy chain. No wonder that St. Paul, raised to the third heaven, and then lowered to earth, should cry from his exile and banishment: 'Cupio dissolvi et esse cum Christo!'*

---

* I desire to be dissolved, and to be with Christ.

50

Face to Face

How keenly that great saint discovered the workings of the spirit is evidenced by that one expression: 'We know in part; and we prophesy in part. We now see through a glass in an obscure manner; but then face to face. Now I know in part; but then I shall know even as I am known.' It is like an interpretation of the shadow on the wall in Plato's cave. But what a boundless horizon of knowledge it opens up after death. 'Face to face.' No longer through the dusk and shadowy intermediary of sense; but confronting the reality, seeing all around it, and through it, and beyond it, discerning the *noumena* beneath the *phenomena* of things, and grasping firmly those shadowy and elusive pictures of substance and form, and space and time and infinity. What a revelation it will be! And what an eternity of happiness, in forever seeking after and finding the eternal and immutable truths, manifested in the vision of God.

Maine de Biran

But how do we touch the extremes, 'the personal ego,' as Maine de Biran says, 'in whom all begins, and the personal God, in whom all ends'? Where is the chain that links these vast extremes of eternity? Let us see. The main organs of the body are automatic, but governed by a mysterious something called Life. The worlds of the Universe are automatic, but governed by a mysterious something called Law. But Life is governably by volition that can conserve or destroy within limitations, and Law is governed by the Supreme Will that can suspend or direct it at pleasure. The organic body and the inorganic universe; Life in the former, Law in the latter. The human volition controlling Life; the Divine volition evolving Law – there is a perfect analogy, so far as the limitations of a Finite and the Absoluteness of an Infinite Being are concerned.

The One Principle

It is a curious law of our intellectual being – that by which we are perpetually striving to unify all laws, and to seek after a First Principle. In the laboratory the scientist is forever seeking after the one great science which is to harmonize all former discoveries, and make future experiments more easy and more successful by the application of one great principle. Poets, too, have dreamed of this eternal and unique One.

The One remains; the many change and pass.

Philosophers have veiled their dim consciousness of it under the name of the Unconditioned and Absolute. But the higher the scientist, the poet, and the philosopher go in their speculations, the nearer they find themselves to the principle of Unity. Yet it is ever elusive and unattainable, vanishing at the moment of touch, then reappearing in the eternal and unquenchable passion of human striving after a unity of law, of principle, of origin, of all things that pass under the names of human cognitions or mental concepts. And so that One ever remains as an eternal and irrefragable principle of philosophic thought, beyond knowledge, but not beyond reason or belief – accessible to thought as a principle – inaccessible in Its attributes and modes; the dread reality of the humble and devout; the persistent and unwelcome visitant which haunts the brain of

process of evolution was perfect, that link was knit to link in the great chain; how is it explained that the mighty process was suddenly stopped at man? He has had plenty of time to have evolved into something higher. The lower forms did not require so much time to develop into the higher; and there is less difference, therefore less of a leap of life and progress, between a man and an angel than between an ape and a man. Yet, Nature stands still. Confucius was as wise as Plato; and Plato greater than Herbert Spencer. Or, is nature, like the mighty suns, going to take a leap backward now? Has she ceased to expand, and has the process of recession begun? And, descending the ladder of creation, is she about to step down from species to species, into the vegetable organism, thence into the molecule, the monad, the atom again?

The Argument from Analogy

Our great mistake is, not in arguing by analogy, but in not pushing analogy far enough in its widest, most expansive sense. One argues about the infinity of inhabited worlds; but forgets that these worlds must be inhabited by beings as different from us as their suns and planets differ from ours. Our sun is but a third-rate star; our planet but a minor off-shoot of nebulae. If all the suns of space have their planets (as we might assume), these latter must have intelligent, self-conscious inhabitants; but if these suns are vastly greater than ours and differ in constitution, density, and brilliancy, so, too, must their satellites differ from our satellites, and their inhabitants from us, until we can not only imagine, but reason about beings as vastly superior to us in intellect, as we suppose angelic intelligences to be; and according to the density of their sphere becoming more and more immaterial, and therefore less liable to dissolution, until at last we touch on the subtlety and swiftness, the mobility and spirituality of our angels; so that we pass by the strictest analogy of evolution from the composite nature of a man to purely spiritual creations, ascending higher and higher in the scale of intellectuality and subtlety, until we touch the fringe of that sea of Spirits that undulates within the precincts of heaven; and there, mount higher and higher, until we reach the nine orders in all their transcendent beauty and perfection, culminating in the glories of the Archangels, who stand sentinels before the 'great white throne'; where, suddenly, we are smitten back to earth by beholding in the innermost sanctuary of the Most High, the Hierarchy of the Incarnation, close by the enveiled Majesty of Him, 'whose throne is darkness,' and yet 'enveloped in light as with a garment.'

Evolution stops at Man

'But all this only argues the existence of demigods.' So said Mill about the cosmological argument of the schools. But even on the theories of the evolutionists we cannot stop here. Not only as a fact in *esse,* but as a creation, yet a logical creation of pure thought, as an intellectual concept arising from a strict intellectual process, evolution cannot stop except with God. You must either accept the Christian idea of God, as originator of the Universe, or God as its ultimate development. He is either Alpha or Omega – the Being from whom all things derive their being; or the Being in whom all things terminate, or according to the Pauline idea – both. For if matter is eternal, it must have been developing and evolving its energies from eternity; and conceding for a moment that Nature can leap the chasm from the inorganic to the organic, we have at last, after countless cycles of years, and endless processes of evolution, this tiny being called Man. Man, the lowest type or rational creature we can conceive, is the ultimate development of the eternal processes of the suns. But man is only a quite recent triumph of evolution. Yesterday he was an ape, the day before a vegetable, the day before a gas! Then what has Nature being doing from eternity? Is this its highest result? Nay, nay, says the agnostic, there must be higher natures than Man's, if matter, with all its potencies, has had eternity to work in. Then you admit the existence of angels? why not the existence of God? The very imperfection of man argues a *direct creation* in what we call Time.

The First, and the Last

Yes, eternity supposes Infinity. An eternity of matter in perpetual repose, inert, inexpansive, unattractive, inoperative, we may conceive, but we know it to be impossible and non-existent. But a dead universe might still be regarded as of indefinite duration and extent. But a Universe, like ours, in perpetual motion of dissolution and creation, of repulsion and assimilation, in a state of perpetual flux and motion, and with the one result of which we are most immediately cognizant, namely – ourselves, sentient and rational beings, demands or foreshadow Infinity. But this time, not the indefinite dead Universe, but an Infinite, if incomprehensible, Mind. For if Mind proceeds from Matter, as Materialists say, it is clear that the operation has not reached its term of possibilities in human intellect. That would be a poor result. But if it can reach higher, why has it not done so? It has had all eternity to work in. Either, then, man is the supreme achievement of Nature, or not. If he is, Nature, perfect in all its other operations, has failed here. If not, and if there be some higher possibilities, then the operations of Nature from all eternity must have produced Infinite Mind. Man can be explained by the theory of direct creation. He is unintelligible by the theory of evolution, except as a chance accident, flung from the crucible of being in a moment of lawless and misguided frenzy. But this, too, won't do; for law is paramount, and admits no errancy or arbitrariness. Then, you cannot assume the existence of man, except by direct creation; for if he is the feeble and halting result of endless processes, working upwards from the womb of eternity, these endless processes in the infinitude of space would have developed something far greater and more worthy of such vast potencies and such illimitable areas of space and time. 'Very well,' says the evolutionist, 'grant our theory, and we have no objection to your placing God at the end of the chain of existence.' But this won't answer, because according to every axiom of philosophy, the conditioned can never develop into the Absolute. We are face to face then with this dilemma – Man, the apex of creation, after countless millions of years; and all the energies of Nature working in an illimitable field; or man, the handiwork of God, yet the lowest in the scale of rational beings. How absurd the former hypothesis – how simple and reasonable and free from embarrassment the latter. 'Who hath wrought and done these things, calling the generations from the beginning? I, the Lord! I am the First and the Last!'*

* Isaiah xli. 4.

The Immateriality of Mind

I think it is in Lewes' *Biographical Dictionary of Philosophy* the words occur: 'I can say, *Cogito, ergo sum;* I cannot say, *Cogito, ergo Deus est.*' Lewes had read the philosophers, but he was never admitted into the sacred circle. 'He hath been to a great feast of thought, and he hath stolen the scraps.' All men are agreed that the first proposition has been disastrous to human thought. But where comes in the unreason of the second proposition? If you admit that man exists and thinks, you necessarily postulate the existence of Supreme Thought – that is, God. Descartes and his school would not accept for a moment that theory of modern Materialists – that thought, mind, soul, are purely material operations or functions. To them thought was evolved by will-power, itself immaterial, and its product became immaterial with it. Then you leap at once with the two concepts of Time and Space, as on two vast wings, to Supreme Immaterial and Inorganic Thought – that is, to God. The Finite can never develop into the Infinite, nor the Conditioned evolve into the Absolute. But it can prove it – nay, demand it. Once admit that thought is immaterial, although requiring an organic substance, in our conditions of being, to evolve it, and you reach, with one sweep of reason – the ultimate, as well as the principle of all thought – God! On the one hand man's very littleness, as unworthy of the dignity of the Universe, foreshadows God; and on the other, the grandeur of his immaterial faculties demands and postulates Supreme Intelligence.

Hegel and Schelling

Yet it is remarkable that the more spiritual or idealistic schools of German philosophy, represented by Hegel and Schelling, are completely at issue with this logical deduction from modern materialism. Their programme in the *Critical Journal* asserts that the 'great immediate interest of philosophy is to put God again absolutely at the head of the system as the one ground of all, the *principium essendi et cognoscendi,* after He has been for a long time placed, either as one infinitude alongside of other infinitudes, or at the end of them all as a postulate – which necessarily implies the absoluteness of the finite.' This reads like a sentence from some mediæval Catholic philosopher, with its Scholastic terminology, until we see further into the Philosophy of Identity – a monistic system which, taking choice between God and the human mind, eliminates the former, or rather amalgamates both under the unmeaning word – Subject-Object. Then comes a schism; and Hegel passes out into the unknown barren deserts of the 'Phenomenology of Spirit,' and Schelling follows with his spiritual Pantheism until, driven back by inexorable logic, he finds reason is God – the only God; and God is reason – the spectre of itself cast by the retina of the soul on the background of Eternity.

Here, too, again we notice one of the striking similarities between the systems and terminology of these stars of the outer darkness and our own great philosophical lights. For here Hegel breaks completely with Schelling, and gives a system of genetic philosophy in which he corresponds, word for word, and idea for idea, with St. Thomas, beginning with the lowest sensuous consciousness and working upwards through reason and experience to the highest speculative thought, and denying that any man has a right to impose his own intuitions, or

60

what he conceives to be his visions, on the acceptance of the world; whilst Schelling reduces all apprehension of truth to each individual's consciousness, or his intuitive perception of all human verities.

The Pathos of Nature

The voice of Nature is a voice of loneliness – the voice of one crying in the wilderness. The autumn winds moaning in the crevices of chimneys; the deep, sad monotone of the sea; the weary plash of rain in the night; the sound of the waterfall from afar; the voice of rivers, deepened from the babble of streams; the moan of the storm in the leafless trees; even the zephyrs amongst the young leaves of spring; – all have an undertone of sadness, as if they too felt the 'burden and the weight of all this unintelligible world.' And here this evening I start and shudder under the 'eldritch light' of an autumn sunset, at the

Low breathings coming after me, and sounds
Of undistinguishable motion, steps
Almost as silent as the turf they trod.

It is only the gentle susurrus of the evening breeze, and the zip! zip! of a red leaf falling into its brown grave. I saw it in the springtime, when it gradually unfolded from its cradle; and fulfilling the universal law, expanded its tiny silken gloss to the sunlight. I saw it, again by universal law, attacked by parasites, which clung to its pale under-side, and left a brown mark of decay after them; I saw it tossed on the storm, wooed by the zephyr, wet with the weeping of the rain and the tears of the dew, shaken by the wanton, careless bird, caressed by the sun, pallid beneath the moon; and now comes its turn, as of all things, to die and fall, and pass into the inorganic kingdom again. But its last sound on earth startled me with its fluttering farewell, and its silent reminder: Thou too shalt pass. It is the law.

A magnetic storm

We had a terrific magnetic storm last night. Wise people who understand the eternal laws of Nature, and the marvellous interdependence of suns and planets, foresaw it. For there were, all this year, spots in the sun, great rents in the photosphere here and there, into whose horrible jaws you might fling thousands of pebbles, such as this little earth of ours, without the chance of satiating them. So I told my little children in the convent schools here. They received the information with a smile of pitying incredulity. Then there were some magnificent Auroras, up there in hyperborean regions – vast plumes of light cast up from an unseen cauldron in the blazing heavens, and stretched out in a great fan of colours, frail and iridescent as a rainbow's. So we said to ourselves: Something is coming. This is but the stage scenery. When will the performance commence? Sure enough, yesterday afternoon there were some deep grumblings in that half bronze, half copper sky, which always holds in its hollows untold terrors. These were the prelude to the mighty nocturnal oratorio of the heavens. It commenced, as oratorios do, ever so softly and gently, a mere susurrus of sound, echoed down along the bases of the black mountains and fading away to invisible distances. But every two seconds the sky was a sheet of blue flame, fitful and flickering, and yet broad and deep and permanent enough to show every outline - leaf, and bough, and trunk, of the belt of forest trees opposite my window, and every ripple in the river beneath. There was no sleeping now. I arose. So did every one in the village except the little children in their innocence, who slept right through the storm: and a tramp, who was drunk. I lighted my candle, and tried to read. It was useless. Those broad, blue flashes, flickering like swallows' wings across my windows, forbade it. There was nothing for it but to witness in awe and with strained nerves the explosion in fire and fury of the elements of heaven.

Its climax

Then it struck me that my stables were in danger. I passed out into the yard to examine them; and so powerful is the force of imagination, I distinctly saw fire flickering across the ridges of some thatched roofs outside my garden walls. Next day, I was surprised to find that these cottages were not burned to the ground. I returned, and sat patiently watching the play of the electric fluid across the heavens and athwart the landscape. Hitherto, no rain had fallen; but about 2 a.m. the flashes became more frequent, as if the whole heavens were a tremendous battery, belching out blue flame at every moment. And the deep diapason of the thunder came nearer, and broke in deeper and longer volleys, reverberating across the valley, and shattered against the black mountains far away. The strain became severe; and I prayed for one drop of rain to certify that Nature was melting away in its own terrific anger. But not a drop, only the swift wings of light beating across sky and earth, and the deep growl of the thunder coming nearer and nearer. Up to this the town was as still as death – still with the silence under which all souls are hushed in terror, as if there were no escape, and nothing remained but to wait and pray. About three o'clock, however, as the storm deepened in intensity, a poor half-demented creature rushed wildly into the streets and cried: 'The town is on fire! the town is on fire!' It was ghastly, that lonely cry in the stillness and dread.

And termination

It was so like the cry of the angels who abandoned Jerusalem in the crisis of its fate: Let us go hence! Let us go hence! But a more startling sound struck the ears of the trembling people. Two poor jennets, who had been out feeding on the highways in defiance of the law, tore madly across the bridge and into the streets, screaming wildly in terror; and their cry resembled so exactly the wail of women, despairing and stricken, that it seemed for a moment as if the whole town had gone mad from fright and rushed like maniacs abroad. At last, about 4 a.m., a few drops of rain fell and I said, Thank God! But the storm was reaching its climax. The blue flashes, broad and gleaming, gave way before the terrific artillery that now broke right above our heads; and great bloodred and forked javelins of fire stabbed here and there through the inky blackness. It was horrible – those fire missiles flung at us we know not from where, and running zigzag, now in the heavens above, now on the earth beneath; and after every flash such a crash of thunder that one could well believe that the end of all things had come; that the fountains of the great deep were broken up; and that Earth and Heaven were rushing together pell-mell into chaos. And the one hope was that the rain was now pouring in a deluge from the skies; and the plash from roof and housetop and gully was almost equal in horror to the weird music in the heavens. At last, about 4.30 a.m., there was a flash of blinding light, as if hell had opened and shut; then a moment's pause, and then such a snarl of sound overhead, such a malignant, fiendish growl, as of a thousand maddened beasts, that I involuntarily put my fingers in my ears and murmured: Eleison! It was the last bar in the great oratorio of the heavens. The sounds rumbled and died far down on the edges of the horizon; the skies cleared; and nought was heard only the unseen cataracts pouring down their floods from the broken reservoirs of heaven.

A few days later I read, with surprise, that this frightful cataclysm was limited to a narrow belt of atmosphere not half a mile in depth. Beyond and above the eternal stars shone peacefully.

Terrible, but limited

About six o'clock the evening before the storm a tramp came into my garden, where I was reading. My servant said: A gentleman wanted to see me! So I said: Send him up. We are so polite in Ireland that everyone is a gentleman or a lady, when they are not noblemen. I saw at a glance at his boots that he was a tramp. Now, I like tramps, just as I like everything planetary and wandering. It is because I am such a precisian that I could not sit down to dinner if a picture was hung awry, or a book misplaced on a shelf, that I love irregularities in others. A piece of torn paper on my carpet will give me a fit of catalepsy; but I can tranquilly contemplate the awful chaos of another's study, and even congratulate him on his splendid nerves. So tramps, comets, variable stars, wandering lights of philosophy, stars of the outer darkness, flotsam and jetsam of heaven and earth – I have a curious sympathy with them all, as fate or fortune blows them about in eccentric orbits. This wayfarer told me he was from my native town (which was a lie); that he was a tradesman out of employment (which was another); that he was hungry and thirsty (which was half-and-half). I gave him sixpence, which he instantly transmuted into whiskey. Then he lay down under an open archway, and slept all through that terrific storm. I have no doubt but that the electric fluid shot through that open arch again and again during the night; but the Eudæmon, who presides over drunken people, warded off the bolts. He woke next morning, stiff, but sound and whole, and was utterly amazed at the universal consternation.

SECTION III.

Christianity the perfect and final Religion

It has often occurred to me that the revelations of Christianity upon human beliefs had much the same effect as fire upon invisible ink. All the vague, shadowy credences of humanity broadened out and glowed in intense light, the outlines of which no longer faded away into undefined and conjectural speculations; but became clearly edged and marked, and indelible. The Elohim drew together and became God, the Spirit. All the ancient trinities– Hindu, Egyptian, or Greek, were defined and determined in the Father, the Son, and the Holy Ghost. And the apotheosis of man, and his supreme excellence, which has always haunted human thought with such a suggestion of pride, that it has created gods after its own image, – reversing the process of creation, – was almost realized when the 'Word was made Flesh, and dwelt amongst us.' And there it remains – this supreme Theogony of Christian revelation. The ever-rebellious mind of man has striven to dissolve it again into the old shadows of verbal abstractions and lofty unrealities. But never again shall the supreme revelation be disturbed. It is written in God's handwriting; and chisel or acid cannot impair its outlines. It is revealed in words that shall not pass, even though the earth, like a worn garment, be cast aside and changed; and the Heavens, like a reader's scroll of parchment, be folded up and hidden away in the archives of eternity.

Modern tendency to Paganism

Hence, human pride is forever revolting against this revelation. The unrestrained intellect is forever beating its wings against this wall of brass, that marks its limitations. It would so like to go out, and wander at its own sweet will across the deserts of the Universe, and build its own idols, as the Israelites, even under God's very eye, built their *simulacra* of gold and silver, and said they were their Gods. Human folly is never at an end. It only takes different modes and shapes. When one thinks of the orgies of the French Revolution, and the apotheosis of Reason under the vilest form conceivable, it seems not too far-fetched to predict that modern civilization may yet revert to the gods of Greece and Rome.

Reversion to Christianity

And, then, when it has wallowed in the sink and sty of uncleanness, its old God-like aspirations, stifled but not extinguished by pride and sensuality, will revive; and it will come back once again to the sweetness and dignity, the celestial graces and eternal hopes of Christianity. There it will find peace, 'clothed and in its right mind' for a time; until the untamable spirit clamours again for the fierce liberties of untrammelled thought and unlimited license; and leaves its vale of Tempe for the howling desert, and the turbid waters of Marah.

Fénelon

What a wonderful camera is the mind! The sensitized plate can only catch the material picture painted by the sunlight. The *tabula rasa* of the mind can build or paint its own pictures from the black letters of a book. Here is a little series that crossed the diorama of imagination this afternoon. A great bishop, reading his own condemnation from his pulpit, and setting fire with his own hand to a pile of his own books there upon the square of his cathedral at Cambrai; and then constructing out of all his wealth a monstrance of gold, the foot of which was a model of his condemned book, which he thus placed under the feet of Christ, so that every time he gave Benediction he proclaimed his own humiliation.

Lacordaire

Number two picture is that of a great preacher of world-wide reputation, going down into the crypts of the *Carmes,* whilst the great cathedral was still echoing with the thunders of his eloquence; and whilst the enthusiastic audience was filing from the doors, and every lip was murmuring: 'Marvellous!' 'Wonderful,' 'Unequalled,' stripping himself bare and scourging his shoulders with the bitter discipline, until it became clogged with his blood, he murmuring, as each lash fell: *'Miserere mei, Deus, secundum magnam misericordiam tuam.'*

The Curé of Ars

Number three is that of a lowly village church, hidden away from civilization in a low-lying valley in the south of France. It is crowded, it is always crowded night and day; and the air is thick with the respiration of hundreds of human beings, who linger and hover about the place, as if they could not tear themselves away. No wonder! There is a saint here. He is the attraction. It is evening. The Angelus has just rung. And a pale, withered, shrunken figure emerges from the sacristy and stands at the altar rails. Insignificant, old, ignorant, his feeble voice scarcely reaches the front bench. There is seated an attentive listener, drinking in with avidity the words of this old parish priest. He is clothed in black and white. He is the mighty preacher of Notre Dame, and he sits, like a child, at the feet of M. Vianney.

Lamennais

Number four is a lonely chateau, hidden deep in the woods of France, away from civilization. It has an only occupant – a lonely man. He wanders all day from room to room, troubled and ill at ease. His mind is a horrible burden to himself. He is a sufferer from a spiritual tetanus. He cannot say: *Peccavi!* nor *Miserere!* He comes to die in the city. Prayers are said for him in every church and convent in France. The Sister by his bedside presents the last hope – the crucifix. He turns aside from the saving mercy and dies – impenitent. Four months later, after he has been buried, like a beast, without rites, his brother arrives in haste at La Chênaie. The rooms are empty. The dead sleep on. The despairing and broken-hearted priest rushes from chamber to chamber, wringing his hands and crying: 'Oh, mon frère! mon frère!'

The latent power of the Priesthood

It is said, the brute creation knows not its power. If it did, it might sweep man from the earth. The same is said of woman; the same of the Moslem, in reference to European civilization; the same of the Tartar hordes. Might we not without disrespect say: The Catholic priesthood knows not its power? If it did, all forms of error should go down before it. The concentrated force of so many thousand intellects, the pick and choice of each nation under heaven, the very flower of civilization, emancipated, too, from all domestic cares, and free to pursue in the domains of thought that subject for which each has the greatest aptitude, should bear down with its energy and impetuosity the tottering fabrics of human ingenuity or folly. Here, as in most other places, are hundreds who, freed from the drudgery of great cities, the mechanical grinding of daily and uninspiring work, are at liberty to devote themselves to any or every branch of literature or science. They resemble nothing so much as the sentinels posted on far steppes on the outskirts of civilization, with no urgent duty except to keep watch and ward over tranquil, because unpeopled, wastes; and to answer, now and again from the guard on its rounds, the eternal question: 'What of the night, watchman? Watchman, what of the night?' 'Ay,' saith someone, pursuing the simile, 'but suppose the guard finds the sentinel with a book, not a musket in his hands, what then?' Well then, the student-sentinel is promptly courtmartialled and shot!

And it was of these, sentinels of the West, that the very unjust and bigoted Mosheim wrote: 'These Irish were lovers of learning, and distinguished themselves in these times of ignorance by the culture of the sciences beyond all the European nations; the first teachers of the scholastic philosophy in Europe, and who, so early as the eighth century, illustrated the doctrines of religion by the principles of philosophy.'

Irreverence

The worst sign of our generation is not that it is stiff-necked, but that it wags the head and is irreverent. The analytical spirit has got hold of the human mind; and will not leave it until the usual cycle of synthesis and faith comes back again. Outside the Church, I searched for it everywhere – this lost spirit of reverence. I sought it in the devout Anglican, hiding his face in his hat, as he knelt in his well-upholstered pew. Alas! He was killing time in studying the name of *its* maker. I sought it among the philosophers, and found that from Diogenes down, they spat at each other from their tubs. I sought it, rather unwisely, in criticism; and found a good man saying that the '*Saturday Review* temperament was ten thousand times more damnable than the worst of Swinburne's skits.' I sought it, still more unwisely, in politics; and read that a very great, good statesman 'would appoint the Devil over the head of Gabriel if he could gain a vote by it.' I went amongst my poets; and heard one call another: 'School-Miss Alfred, out-babying Wordsworth and out-glittering Keats;' and the babe replying:

What – is it you
The padded man that wears the stays –

Who killed the girls and thrilled the boys
 With dandy pathos when you wrote?
A lion, you, that made a noise,
 And shook a mane, *en papillotes*.

What profits now to understand
 The merits of a spotless shirt –
A dapper boot – a little hand –
 If half the little soul is dirt?

A Timon you! Nay, nay, for shame!
 It looks too arrogant a jest!
The fierce old man – to take his name,
 You band-box. Off and let him rest!

Then I went away. I passed by France, the cradle of
irreverence, and went out from Occidental civilization.
In the East, the land of the sun, the home of traditional
reverences, the place of all dignity and ceremonial,
where you put the shoes off your feet and touch your
forehead, and place the foot of your master on your
head – here is reverence – the turning to Mecca, the
kissing of the black ruby in its silver sheath in the Kaaba,
and the glory of being an El Hadj; the drinking of the
sacred fountain, *Zem-Zem;* the deep voice of the
preacher: *Labbaika! Allahamma! Labbaika!* I entered
a Turkish town in the evening. The natives had covered
their garments under the *ir'ham,* the vestment of prayer;
the muezzins were calling from the minarets. I watched
one – a young Child of the Prophet – as he seemed to
swing in his cradle high up on the yellow minaret, and
shouted with a voice like that of the Angel of Judg-
ment the invitation to evening prayer. As he swayed to
and fro in that lofty nest, his face seemed lighted with

a kind of ecstatic solemnity, as it shone in the rays of the declining day.

It was the perfection of prayer and reverence. The setting sun, the long shadows, the face to the East, the silence, the decorum, and the prophetic voice from the clouds. Alas! I saw a grave father thumping the young prophet on the back when he descended; and the young prophet winked with an expression: 'Didn't I do it well?' Alas, for the Prophet! Alas, for Allah, Il-allah! He was calling to a *Yashmak* down there in the street!

Reverence

On the other hand, I find the summit of reverence touched by two extremes in Catholicity – the Cistercian, sitting with folded hands before the oakbound, brass-hefted Ordinal in the choir; and the little Irish children in our convent schools at prayer. The former is the culmination of religious dignity and reverence; the latter of Christian simplicity and reverence. And it would be difficult to say which of the two is the more pleasing in Heaven's sight. But whether the heavy doors of the Kingdom would swing open more lightly under the strong and vigorous push of the Trappist, or the light, soft, timid touch of the child, one thing is certain, that the Angels might claim kinship with either in that supreme matter of reverence. And I suppose this is the reason why, in the two most pathetic instances narrated in Holy Writ, where the vengeance of God had to be averted from His people, in the one case the priests of the Lord stood weeping between the people and the altar, and in the other the prostrate figures of little children strewed the sanctuary before the face of the Most High.

The Pearl of great Price

Once upon a time, in the great city of Cairo, when the markets were full of busy merchants, and the narrow streets were loaded with merchandise, a Dervish came in from the desert, and, looking meekly around for a vacant space in the crowded mart, he laid down his square of carpet, and knelt and prayed. He then unfolded his garments, and placed on the carpet a tiny box, but it contained a pearl of great price. The passersby laughed at the poverty of his belongings, and the great merchants, who sold spices and silks and unguents, turned around from time to time and jeered at the Dervish and his little paper box. No one came to buy nor ask his price, and he remained all day, his head silently bent in prayer. His thoughts were with Allah! Late in the evening, as the asses of the rich merchants passed by, laden with costly goods, they came and sniffed at the little box that held the rich pearl. Then, lifting their heads in the air, they brayed loudly: 'It is not hay! It is not hay!' And some grew angry, and cried still louder: 'Give us hay! It is not hay!' Now, the holy man said not a word. But when the sun had set, and nearly all had departed, he took up his box and hid it away in the folds of his garments, and, kneeling, he prayed. Then he gathered up his square of carpet, and passed out into the desert, saying in his heart: 'Blessed be Allah, Il-Allah!' And afar on the night-winds he heard the bray of the market-asses: 'It is not hay! It is not hay! Give us hay!'

The Excellence of Philosophy

This is the chief excellence and attraction of philosophy. It is an inexact science. One is always seeking the insoluble – going out into unknown regions after the Inexplicable and Undefined. Other sciences hand over to you their coins stamped and minted with the face or sigil of their kings; philosophy is not a *minted coin,* but an inexhaustible mine of all precious thoughts and sublime principles. It deals with abstractions; and to the end of time it is the abstract that will enchain the powers of that eternal Inquisitor – the Human Mind. Hence the great philosophers stand head and shoulders over all others in the vast Acropolis of human knowledge. Warriors, and statesmen and orators, artists in words, or marble, or canvas, sit at the feet of the priests of Pallas; and draw thence their inspiration. Greece is Greece because of its philosophy. Nay, nay, some one says, Greece is Greece for its Homer and Æschylus, for Pheidias and Pericles, for Themistocles and Leonidas! Yes, but where was the fountainhead of all this inspiration – poetical, patriotic, artistic? Was it not in that philosophy, imported from India; and which, personifying the best conceptions of the human mind in the form of deities and demigods, created for dramatist, sculptor and painter, the noble archetypes of their ideas and works; and gave to her patriots the inspirement that in defending, or exalting their country, they earned the favour of the gods, and the guerdon of an immortality to be shared with them on Olympus or in the Elysian fields?

Ancient Rome imported its Philosophy

So ancient Rome is barren of immortals, because Rome was the school-room of imported sophists, not the cradle or home of original thought. Rome had never a philosophy. The spirit of Greece hovered around her coasts wherever the subtle-minded children of Attica or Asiatic Greece found a temporary refuge; and the Roman spirit, accustomed to the direct and violent arbitrament of the sword or mace, never took kindly to the subleties of dialectics, or the nebular speculations of the aliens. They possessed the earth; and they did not want the sky. They held the realities of life; and dispensed with the dreams. They solved riddles in their own way. But, as a consequence, whatever of art they possessed was imported; their great temples were Grecian; Corinthian columns supported their forums and palaces; their greatest poem dealt with a Grecian hero; and their greatest orator derived all his graces of diction and all the subtleties of his eloquence from Grecian models, whose inspiration he never acknowledged, possibly because in the translation into his own speech it was diluted into the thinnest of rhetoric and the most vapoury in suggestion or reflection.

The Greek Fathers

The Greek Fathers, too, unquestionably lord it over the Latins (always excepting St. Augustine, who if not a Platonist, was decidedly Platonic), at least in two things – subtlety of thought and sweetness of expression. Whether it was the genius of the language, which having served to embody the greatest poetry in the world, has now descended to become the handmaid of science, or the effect of climate or ethnical conditions, there is no doubt that the Greek Patristic writings are fuller of rhetorical grace, and suggestive elegances than the Latin. The latter perhaps gain somewhat in strength and precision from this very absence of grace and beauty of expression. But one can well understand how the compilers of Anthologies or Excerpts would select the former as richer in thought and sweeter in expression, and therefore more representative of what the early Church might have been in system and spirit. So speculative truth was never alienated from practical wisdom. Both combined to form the theogony of the Eastern Church. And both, strange to say, rested on Plato and Aristotle combined. For, to quote an expression of Coleridge, 'in wonder (τῷ θαυμάζειν) says Aristotle, does philosophy begin; and in astonishment (τῷ θαμβεῖν) says Plato, does all true philosophy finish.' And it was in this union of theology and philosophy, indigenous to Greek thought, that the special excellence of the Greek Patristic writings consist.

Cycles of Thought

It is very doubtful if there be a single idea in modern philosophy that was not borrowed from the ancients. The atomic theory, the theory of monads, archetypal and ectypal ideas, Pantheism in its Protean forms – all were familiar to Pythagoreans and Eleatics; as they are to us. For al philosophy resolves itself into belief in one of three theories: –

Dualism.	(a) Mind alone exists – Idealism – the Pantheism of Hegel and Schelling.
	(b) Matter alone exists – Materialism – the Pantheism of Spinoza.

Monism. $\left\{\begin{array}{l}\end{array}\right.$ *(c)* Mind and Matter exist – Christian Theism.

And, if we study the ancient schools, and at the same time accept St. Augustine's bold idea, that Christianity did exist, even though as a penumbra and faintly, before Christ, we shall find that human thought, instead of moving in a straight line towards the insoluble problem of existence, is really turning round and round in concentric circles.

Adumbrations of Christianity

Was not the fall of man known to Empedocles:
τρίς μυριάς ὥρας· ἀπὸ μακάρων ἀλαλῆσδαι,
and the absolute necessity for καθάρμοι, expiations; and was not the Trinity known to the Platonists:
περὶ τριῶν ἐξ ἑνος ὑποστάντων
and
Τὸ αὐτὸ "ON
Τὸν δεμιουργόν Λόγον, or Νοῦν, καί
Τὴν τοῦ κόσμου Ψυχήν.

And if we have seen before that man's mind tends naturally to the One Supreme Being, or Cause, and one Supreme Law, so, too, the tremendous mystery of the Trinity, before which the Church veils her face with an O, Altitudo! has haunted all philosophical thought from the beginning. But perhaps the most extraordinary manifestation is in the systems of two such cometary lights as Hegel and Schelling. Both of these philosophers seem to trace a trinity of action and interaction in all nature, working upwards from incipient consciousness to the great mystery, which, alas! they leave in abeyance. We place these trinities of thought side by side, to show

how fantastically the greatest minds can operate on theoretic assumptions; and also to show what strange dementia has passed into the history of what is called Philosophy.

HEGEL.

The Idea. – Three elements:
1. – In itself.
2. – In opposition to contrary idea.
3. – In union with it.

or

1. – The Idea in itself.
2. – Out of itself.
3. – Into, or for itself.

The Faculties: –
1. – The Perception of the Senses.
2. – The Understanding that divides perception.
3. – The Reason that unites.

The Sciences: –
1. – Logic.
2. – The Philosophy of Nature.
3. – The Philosophy of Mind.

The Religions: –
1. – The Oriental Religion.
2. – The Greek Religion.
3. – The Christian Religion.

Union of Philosophy and Religion: –
1. – In the Christian community at its beginning.
2. – In the Organized Church.
3. – In the State.

SCHELLING.

The Potencies: –
1. – (Potenz der Reflexion) Reflective Movement.
2. – (Potenz der Subsumption) Subsumptive Movement.
3. – (Potenz der Vernunft) Reasoning Movement.

These potencies are exercised thus:
On Matter:
1. – Expansion.
2. – Attraction.
3. – Gravity.

In Dynamics:
1. – Magnetism.
2. – Electricity.
3. – Galvanism.

On Organisms:
1. – Reproduction.
2. – Irritability.
3. – Sensibility.

The same three potencies are exercised
On Mind – In Knowledge:
1. – Sensation.
2. – Reflection.
3. – Freedom.

In Action:
1. – The Individual.
2. – The State.
3. – History.

Finally the two philosophers agree on three great
cardinal principles:
1. – The identity of Thought and Being.
2. – The identity of Contradictories.

3. – The *processus* of things, making the human
mind the ultimate term.

No wonder that a French writer, after the study of these
'weird speculations,' should say: –

I must frankly confess that my first sentiment as I leave
these strange speculations of modern Germany is one of
astonishment, that in the country of Leibniz they should
have been able to enthrall men's minds so long.

The Gospel – The Term of all Philosophies

But, with all that incongruity and utter unreasonableness,
it is certain that what are called Hegelians of the Right
would find their conclusions lead infallibly into the
dogmatism of the Catholic Church, just as the 'identity
of contradictories' seems to be found in the highest
ethics of Christian faith; and Schelling's Pantheism,
crude and blasphemous, is but the truncated and un-
developed form of Christian mysticism. So that all
philosophy, after passing through the tortuous mazes
of human speculative thought, emerges in the Gospel;
just as the wildest theories of existence, and thought, and
being, terminate in the Eternal, Self-Existent cause!

A friendly Robin

I was pulling up some withered asters to-day. A robin
came over in a friendly way and looked on. I was
grateful for the pretty companionship. It was familiar,
and I hate stand-off and stuck-up people. I knew he
admired my industry, if not my skill. He looked very

pretty with his deep-brown back, and scarlet breast-plate, and his round wondering eyes watching mine. Alas, no! he was watching something else. A rich, red, fat worm wriggled from the roots of the dead flowers. Robin instantly seized him, flung him down, bit him in halves, then in quarters; then gobbled up each luscious and living morsel, and looked quite innocent and un-concerned after the feat. He had swallowed as much raw meat as a grown man who would dine off three or four pounds of beefsteak; and he was his own butcher. And this is the wretch that poets rave about!

His Song

But hark! that ripple, that cascade of silver sound, as if from the throat of an angel! Not the shrill continuous anthem of the lark, as he shivers with the tremulous raptures of all the music in him; nor the deep bell-tones of the blackbird, as on a May morning he makes all the young forest leaves vibrate with the strong, swift waves of his melody; but a little silver peal of bells on a frosty morning. Who is it? What is it? An Oread from the mountains, who has lost her way hither; or a Hama-dryad from yonder forest who is drawing out her wet tresses after her revel in the silver cascade? No, but that butcher, that cannibal – that glutton! I'll begin soon to believe that prima-donnas drink; and that poets eat like mortals.

Keats

No, no! In spite of this horrible disillusion I will not, I cannot believe that Keats, Keats of the 'Hyperion,' Keats of 'The Ode to the Nightingale,' Keats of the immortal sonnet, did actually and verily get drunk for six weeks together. Can you even conjecture it, that the Greek dreamer who saw such wonders in the Grecian urn, and who looked through the

Magic casements opening on the foam
Of perilous seas in fairy lands forlorn,

did actually scorch his palate with cayenne pepper in order to enjoy all the more the cool deliciousness of claret? And yet it is not incredible. His letters about Fanny Brawne, and to her, reveal a strong sensuous soul, a fitting counterpart to his Charmian, – a Roman, not a Greek, – epicurean, Pagan, unrestrained, incontinent; and all in the frailest body that was ever hung together by the subtlest threads of an immortal spirit. There, my robin has flown with his worm!

'Mad Shelley'

And 'mad Shelley!' The first of English lyrists. Nay, nay, I cannot retract, if it is a literary heresy a hundred times over. I place him high up there on the shelf, side by side, nay, even above Shakspere. 'There is a good deal of lying about Shakspere,' says a certain distinguished American. So there is! Goethe commenced it in that very silly and salacious book, *Wilhelm Meister's Apprenticeship*. Some day men may assure themselves on irrefragable evidence that Francis Bacon and William Shakspere were one and the same person; and that Francis Bacon was not a great philosopher, nor an original thinker (that is conceded already); and that William Shakspere, the greatest of dramatists, is not the greatest of poets. The greatest interpreter of the human; the poorest interpreter of the divine, was Shakspere. But Shelley! Like his own skylark, he never leaves the skies. At least he never sings on earth. He is a denizen of the empyrean. He lives in clouds and lightning, and walks on their upper floors. He has his feet on the shoulders of the winds, and is the pilgrim of darkness and solitude. He has not thought one weak thought, nor written one dull line. His soul is 'girt by the deserts of the universe'; and he seems to ascend, in the flesh, to the soul of some planet, that

> Swings silent in unascended majesty.

He is poet of high thought, the prophet of abstractions, the magician, who impersonates on canvas the impersonal and abstract; and fills his pages and the universe with all kinds of spiritual and transcendent creations. And yet, there is his apology for free love and atheism; and there is that hideous blasphemy, which should make every line he wrote worthy to be burnt by a public hangman, and their incinerated relics cast into the common sewer; and yes! there is the body of Harriet Westbrook dragged from the slime of the Serpentine, and he with Mary Goodwin and Claire Clairmont over there in the Capri of the Villa d'Allegri. Alas! there is the robin and the worm again!

His Philanthropy

Nevertheless, turn away your imagination for a moment from the 'mad Shelley' of Eton and *Queen Mab;* of Harriet Westbrook and Claire Clairmont; and try and see only the Shelley who took the epileptic woman in his arms to the friend's house; the Shelly who never touched meat nor wine; who lay for hours with his head near the blazing fire, or on the burning roofs of Pisa; who chased the flying Allegra through the convent cloisters, and saw her rising from the sea; who gave away every fraction of money he possessed; who went down to his sea-death, and seemed to his friends to hover above the furnace or crematory on the Italian sands; then recall the music as of Ariel in his incomparable lyrics; the choral anthems in his great dramas; his odes to the Skylark and the West Wind, and you reluctantly declare that he was the ἐσ σ άμενος πυριπύρ, if ever there was one.

Well, well, how easy it is to forget the mangled worm in the song and plumage of the bird!

A singular union

Is there an explanation of this most singular blending in one soul of such ethereal purity and such infernal and sordid malignity? How did the mind that followed the skylark into the immaculate recesses of clouds and sunsets, fling up the volcanic and destructive scoriae of the *Revolt of Islam* and *Queen Mab*? He tells us in his pathetic letters to his alarmed publishers: 'I write for the συνετοί ! You might as well go to a ginshop for a leg of mutton as expect anything human or earthly from me.' And then: 'I do not think that twenty will read my "Prometheus!" ' What gave such a spirit this bias towards anarchy and every kind of moral and social and spiritual lawlessness? One can conceive Shelley, trained otherwise, becoming the poet of all sweet and elevated and aspiring souls. Alas! now we have to anthologize him carefully; and look closely between the purple and golden leaves of the culled and fragrant flowers to see

86

that no deadly, though beautiful, serpent lies coiled there. His is the too common and terrible creation – a fair spirit in a woman's form, trailing away into the scaly coils of a snake!

The Fall of the Leaf

Some fine people, or, at least some people who affect fine tastes, despise the dahlia. Not so I. It is a faithful hardy servitor, remaining with us, through the universal abandonment, to the last. Long ago the geraniums have disappeared in cuttings; the red and yellow bells of the begonias have strewn the brown beds; the chrysanthemums with their fragile, cut-paper leaves, are hiding away in the greenhouse. The dahlia, quite independent of autumnal winds, hangs its rich carmine and purple head, full of oval chalices; or flaunts its great star-discs of scarlet flowers in the rich wilderness of leaves. And down comes leaf after leaf into its wintry grave, sometimes falling gently as a consumptive patient passes away; sometimes blown to death by the:

Wild West Wind, the breath of Autumn's being.

Yes, indeed! my horizon is belted rather closer and nearer than I like by the mighty foliage of woods and plantations. This cuts away all view of the blue mountains I should like to see. And in the deep sleep of summer peace, it is rather choking in its profusion and proximity. Nevertheless, it has its advantages – not the least, that it faces, like a strong phalanx, the swift march of the West Wind; and out of the collision and the struggle come sounds of battle that are inspiring, the clash of host upon host, the shout of the advancing battalions, the defiance of the resisting legions. But down they fall in myriads, the slain of the autumnal fight; and the forests will be stripped naked and subdued; and the winter storms with all their ferocity will sweep soundless through the naked and quivering branches. But that wild West Wind, rainless and deepening the shadows of the already closing night, – how it suggests spirits and the dead who live! At least these sombre October evenings I become almost painfully aware of the immediate presence of the dead. Strange I never feel the proximity of father or mother; but my sisters – one in particular, the only dark-haired in the family – has haunted me through life. I no more doubt of her presence and her light touch on the issues of my life than I doubt of the breath of the wind that flutters the tassel of my biretta in my hand. Yet what is strange is not her nearness, but her farness. I should not be in the least surprised if I saw her face shining swiftly from the darkness, or saw her form outlined against the twilight sky. But why I cannot speak to her, or touch her, there is the problem and the vexation.

Behind the veil

And yet, when one comes to think of it, it is seen that such a revelation would destroy all the zest of life by solving too easily the ever interesting enigma. God's wiser ways demand our faith, were it only for our own sake. If all were revealed, all would be commonplace. It is better to believe and hope than to see. If that sister's face did flash suddenly out of the unknown and become so real that I could recognize its spiritual features, would it increase my faith or better my life? Alas, no! After the shock of surprise I might treat it as a delusion of sense. Wisely has the Evangelist put his finger on the lips of Lazarus. If we had been told what he experienced in eternity – would the world believe? No; the world would laugh and go its way.

The Future unknown and merciful

So, too, with that mercy from on high that veils our future in impenetrable mists. Physical science has done a great deal; the occult sciences are now moving forward to take their place. The weather can be forecast. Meteorologists can wire from place to place the depression that foretells a hurricane. But no man can tell me what will occur to me within an hour, a day, a year. And would I seek to know it, if the possibility of such a revelation were at my disposal? No! I would drag the veil faster down on the arcana of the future, and walk forward boldly, holding the hand of God. I will not tempt the future, for I see what a miserable life would have been mine could I have foreseen the vicissitudes of the past. Nor will I fret or be anxious about what may never be. The worst evils are those which never occur. And where would be our faith in Providence – the Far-seer – if our weak eyes could penetrate the dusk of the way we shall have yet to walk?

The Death of Nature

My flowers have lingered patiently all along the dull autumn days, keeping their colours bright under the grey skies and sombre surroundings. The gladioli put out of their sheaths their superb blossoms, like convoluted vases of the richest Venetian glass; the asters held up their faces to their sister stars; the great rich dahlias filled their purple honeycombs with rain and dew; but all seemed anxious to adorn the mother earth from which they sprang, and loth to leave the soft autumnal air and the sweet caresses of wind and soft, pure rain. Last night, however, came a frost, a bitter frost, and all now is wilted and withered unto death. Nothing has escaped. The leaves are black in their decay; the flowers hang their stricken heads. All is over. The pomp of summer and the glory of autumn are at an end. The *hortus conclusus* is now a *hortus siccus* until the time of the snow-drop and the crocus comes again!

Its skeleton framework

This year has died, like a lusty old man who drops off suddenly, retaining his vigour to the last, and putting off decay to the silent metamorphosis of the tomb. The trees had refused to change colour until the final days of October; but then, with a suddenness which made the change more vivid, they put on all the varied colours of smouldering fires, carmine, and umber, and ochre. It was not the burial, but the cremation of Nature. It was intensely beautiful; and there was a look of silent patience in these smouldering forests that made their dissolution intensely pathetic. And low skies, barred with deep grey banks of clouds, between whose parallel ridges, not the sun, but a dim sunlight shone, leaned down over the dying landscape until evening, when the grey melancholy lifted a little, only to show the greater sadness of death, lighted by that lingering sunset. Then, one day, a fierce autumnal hurricane sped out of the red regions of the west; and at night the *mise-en-scène*

of Nature was over; all the purple trappings with which
she had clothed herself for her final valediction and
stage-farewell were flung aside; and there remained only
the skeleton framework of stage and wings, where she
had acted so pompous and so picturesque a part.

A little child

To-day a child in its mother's arms came into my
garden. I looked at it, and saw at the same time the
necessity of the Incarnation. God could not resist taking
that loveliest form – the highest to which material things
have reached. The yellow curls, thick and close and
fine as silk floss, falling down upon his neck; the clear,
limpid eyes, beaming with pure delight; the white teeth,
and his ineffable joy as he played at hide-and-seek behind his mother's neck; and then, becoming suddenly
serious, stroked his mother's cheek, and stared at her
with eyes of wonder! No! If God has chosen to unite
Himself to His creation, He could not have chosen a
lowlier nor a lovelier form. How beautifully these
mediæval painters interpreted this mystery of the Human
and Divine! And with what theological exactitude, yet
with what artistic and withal sympathetic instincts, they
drew from the deep wells of imagination and devotion
their Madonna and Child. Was it Tennyson that found
fault with the serious look in the Child's eyes in that
eighth wonder of the world – the Sistine Madonna?
Look more closely, O poet, and you will find that
Raffaelle was right.

The form of a slave

I cannot agree with the theologians who say that God united Himself to man as His highest rational creature. Man is the lowest in the scale of rational beings. You cannot conceive lower without drifting into the regions of monsters. It was because man was the lowest reason in the scale of creation that God chose to join extremes – to knit Himself, the highest link with the lowest. 'He emptied Himself, taking the form of a slave.'

The temples of the Holy Ghost

But mark the swift and sudden transformation of the creature! 'Remember that thou art but dust, and unto dust thou shalt return!' What a gulf between that ruthless sentence and this – 'Know you not that your bodies are the temples of the Holy Ghost?' What wrought the change in the inspired pages?

The Incarnation!

The Word was made Flesh

I never could understand that mediæval idea of the worthlessness and contemptibility of the body. It was easy to understand it under the Old Law, or by the light of reason alone. But, by the light of Revelation, and in view of the stupendous fact that God chose it as the dwelling-place of His Son on earth, and His eternal, if glorified and transcendent Tabernacle in Heaven, it seems almost a denial of that ineffable mystery to speak of the body as a 'sewer of filth,' 'a tabernacle of corruption,' etc. Viewed in itself it is true that its marvellous and miraculous construction – the adaptability of each organ to its wants, the subtle and complex mechanism, awake enthusiasm in the scientist. The eye alone is a concentrated omniscience, so small in compass, so vast in comprehensiveness and power. But all is mortal and frail. It is but the solidifying of a few gases, that are dissolved in the putrefaction of death. What then? Science says it is a miracle, an eternal and inexhaustible wonder. But science also says it is but a passing whim of restless, constructive Nature – a delusion, a dream, a vapour, a myth. The ancient Scriptures seem to declare the same, but hark! here is a new Revelation, that apotheosizes this figment of clay, and clothes corruption with incorruption. What is the key of the new dogma? *Et verbum Caro factum est!*

THE LONELINESS OF WINTER
by Canon Sheehan

The best-loved of all Irish novelists, it is sometimes forgotten that Canon Sheehan was also a critic, a commentator, and a philosopher, concerned with all the great issues that still obsess men as deeply as they did in the nineteenth century when he wrote his books.

Here he confronts his material directly, discarding the mask of the novelist. He discusses the Psalms; Cardinal Newman; compares De Quincey with Richter and Saint Augustine with Maine de Biran; surprises us with Thomas Carlyle's views on the Mass; reminds us of the vision of Boethius; and, perhaps most significantly of all, finds inspiration in the pensees of Pascal. He writes of the great philosophers Kant and Fichte – not, to our surprise and delight, in abstract terms, but telling the all too human story of Kant's refusal to help Fichte return to his native province.

Both the novelist's sense of drama and the priest's compassion are implicit in his account of a hospital he visited. He reminds us how fortunate we are to be in good health – even to be alive. For a tormented moment he evokes a world of pain and decay – 'that little nodule of flesh is incipient cancer, that flush and chill is typhus, that sudden pain in your left arm is cardiac trouble –' and we remember how thin was the crust that divided the comfortable surface of Victorian life from the threat of disease and death.

But soon he has put gloom behind him and he is writing in a mood of perfect serenity of 'this great red moon, burning through the latticed trees and then paling away as it mounted higher and higher in heaven, was a symbol of the perfect beauty to which all things tend...' His love of nature and his poetic sense of its beauties never fail him. *The Loneliness of Winter* reflects that love; it reflects also Canon Sheehan's understanding of man and of his total dependence on the love of God.

85342 330 x   60p

THE MAGIC OF SPRING
by Canon Sheehan

Canon Sheehan's unique fame as the best-loved of Irish storytellers has obscured the fact that he was a thinker and social critic as well as a creative artist. In fact, he was the forerunner of the modern Catholic novelists: as concerned as they are with man facing a spiritual and intellectual crisis that may change in externals but remains the same in essence.

Here, in a book that combines the quiet mood of the essayist with the insight of the novelist, Canon Sheehan finds some virtue and considerable fascination in everything he discusses. His range is immense: Cato and Dante; the characters of Dickens; the morality of Goethe; Stevenson and Robert Browning – these are only a few of his topics. He tells again the story of the pathetic meeting between the philosopher Bishop Berkeley and the Oratorian Malebranche in Paris; and one can sense his novelist's romantic feeling for disorder when he discusses the canonisation of Saint Benedict Joseph Labre in 1883. Canon Sheehan exults in the paradox of 'this beggar, this tramp with just enough rags to cover him but not to protect him, raised on the alters of the Church for the veneration of the faithful!' He describes how the saint rejoiced that men shrank from him and loathed him; how he sought humiliation 'as fools seek honours'.

The novelist's imagination comes to the fore in his description of a fire: a vivid account of the burning of a great mill, a conflagration so vast that 'the clouds overhead were reddened as in a winter sunset, when the light falls lurid and glaring. The shadows were deep and black; a strange colour tinted hyacinth, tulip, and daffodil in the same monastic and uniform tint.'

The Magic of Spring is a work of great variety, coloured by Canon Sheehan's keen perception of nature, his love of man, and his awareness of God.

85342 327 x   60p

THE BEAUTY OF SUMMER
by *Canon Sheehan*

The best-loved and certainly the most underrated of Irish novelists, Canon Sheehan was more than a novelist. He was a thinker, a social critic, and in the widest sense a philosopher, concerned with all the great questions that have faced man since he first began to think for himself.

This book still offers us Canon Sheehan the master storyteller, but not telling a story; now he meets us face to face and everything that interests him, he contrives to make fascinating to us. He talks of Novalis, and Tolstoy, and Ibsen. He discusses the enigmatic figure of the great Francis Bacon. He evokes the pathetic vision of the German poet Heine rising, semi-paralysed and almost blind, from his matress bed in the Rue d'Amsterdam to pay his last visit to the Venus de Milo in the Louvre – the final obeisance to Beauty from one who had sought it all his life. And in what must strike every reader as a remarkable feat of prophecy, Canon Sheehan assesses the effect of modern Humanism on Irish life.

His passion for suffering humanity is fired by his visit to a penal settlement on a remote island. He and another priest were to hear the confessions of the convicts – 'the summer sun was streaming across the bay, lighting up the headlands all around and the deep hulls of the ships, and casting great long shadows...' But if all was sunshine outside, all was darkness and desolation within. The convicts lived like wild beasts in cages, tier after tier of them, with a net of strong wire in front of each cage, and it was through this that a little air, a little light penetrated. He goes on to contrast the hideous isolation in which the convicts lived with the serene loneliness of the Cistercian monks with whom he stayed a few nights later.

In lighter mood he writes of the false dawn when sleepy little birds wake up reluctantly and ask each other if it is day; and then of the true dawn, when 'all the woods are vocal with the deep rich music of blackbirds and thrushes... let us keep the heart of the morning with its gladness and make of the melancholy of twilight a palinode of the music of the dawn.'

The Beauty of Summer is a book at once lyrical and realistic, the work of a man who saw reflected in nature and his fellow men his own love of God.

85342 328 8   60p

First published in the Netherlands.
Made and printed in Holland by Van Boekhoven-Bosch nv, Utrecht